THE ULTIMATE GUIDE TO AN
EXTRAORDINARY
SERVICE BUSINESS

How to unlock the full potential of your service business

Robert M James

WRITINGMATTERS

The Ultimate Guide To An Extraordinary Service Business

First published in May 2019

Writing Matters Publishing (UK)

info@writingmatterspublishing.com

www.writingmatterspublishing.com

ISBN 978-1-912774-25-8 (Pbk)

Disclaimer: *The Ultimate Guide To An Extraordinary Service Business* is intended for information and education purposes only. This book does not constitute specific advice unique to your situation.

The views and opinions expressed in this book are those of the author and do not reflect those of the Publisher and Resellers, who accept no responsibility for loss, damage or injury to persons or their belongings as a direct or indirect result of reading this book.

All people mentioned in case studies have been used with permission, and have had names, genders, industries and personal details altered to protect client confidentiality and privacy. Any resemblance to persons living or dead is purely coincidental.

Contents

At A Glance

Robert James built *James' Home Services,* from an idea into one of Australia's largest home services franchise operations with over 400 franchisees and annual revenues of over $20million.

In *The Ultimate Guide To An Extraordinary Service Business* Robert gives proven steps to building a successful home services business from scratch.

The 9 Foundations Steps

Robert James developed a proven nine-step system to building a robust service business that includes:

1. Design Your Brand

2. Market Your Business Every Day

3. Get The First Job

4. Always Deliver On Your Promises

5. Organise Your Business

6. Follow-Up with Your Clients

7. Continue To Deliver

8. Ask For The Referral

9. Repeat The Process

Franchisee's paid considerable initial and ongoing fees to have access to these foundation steps because they consistently returned on the investment many times over.

For those who choose to use them, the *9 Foundation Steps* will create extraordinary home service businesses.

For the first time Robert James publicly unpacks the nine steps in detail and he has also added invaluable additional advice supported by case studies.

In addition James explains how to develop systems that will enable your business to grow and scale.

Introduction

If anyone told me back in high school, that by the age of 27 years old, I would be the owner of a home services franchise network, I never would have believed them. Honestly, I would have thought they were completely out of their minds!

I hated school, couldn't wait to get out, and truly didn't see myself as a business leader. I had absolutely no desire to go into the *corporate world*.

I could never have imagined that I would take my part-time, one-man band car cleaning business into a national brand, *James Home Services*. Or that it would grow into a 400-franchisee strong network supplying over $20 million in professional home services annually, for nearly 20 years.

I was just a kid with a horse obsession—I dreamt of being a world-class horse trainer and escaping to beautiful Queensland, Australia to pursue a business career in the race-horse industry.

At 16 years old, I was off chasing my dream and learning as much as possible about the training, breaking, and education of horses; I lived to be around these beautiful creatures!

I had natural horsemanship skills that very few possess and went searching for the adventure of a lifetime.

By the age of 21, I had my professional trainers' license. I had focused on learning absolutely everything about horses and the skills needed to get the best out of them. I was very good at what I did; I was a gifted horseman.

I could read the animal and understand what they needed. In addition, I was lucky enough to have excellent mentors that taught me all about preparing horses for racing.

Unfortunately, what I didn't learn was how to run a business. I was naïve, and thought good horsemanship was all that mattered. If I was the best in the business, then people would be begging me to help them train their horses. What I didn't know was that it was much more about running a business—a racing stable business.

I had not learned any actual business skills and I really, honestly did think that if I was good enough, if I worked hard enough, it would all just miraculously come together.

Most business owners think exactly the same way I did— that it is all about the technical skills. If you are the best horse trainer, mechanic, house cleaner, lawn mower, lawyer, accountant, engineer, or pet groomer, then obviously your business success is guaranteed. Right?

I could not have been more wrong …

This is the first mistake made by most business owners. Good technical skills are only a part of the foundations that create an extraordinary service business.

My horse business started out alright. I had some contacts that became some of my best clients. In the early days, I had some big milestones and was certainly living my dream.

I loved it, but the problem was, I also had a young family to feed and the horse business could be up and down. I needed to find a secondary income.

So, I took an *opportunity* I was offered at a local pub to do some shifts. It was a nightmare; I was terrible at it and I resigned at the end of my first shift.

I was stunned by how rude customers could be.

To this day, I have huge respect for those working in these areas. No way was I going to work in that environment.

A friend then randomly recommended that I consider starting a car cleaning business. He said the guy he usually used was so busy that he couldn't fit him in and, that I could work in the middle of the day around my horse training business.

He would be my first client, actually. I respected his opinion, I knew I could learn to clean a car professionally, much easier than training horses. So, why not?

And with that conversation, my car cleaning business was born. It filled my days and helped to feed my young, growing family. I was 23 years old, had a wife (who also worked), two young sons and two businesses. But you know what? I still hadn't figured out how to run a business.

I still thought it would just happen, how hard could it be to get people that wanted to get their car cleaned? There were heaps of dirty cars around, and I was going to be the best! Easy, right?

Well ... I did do a few things right though. First, I found a guy who sold car cleaning chemicals and equipment and really knew his stuff. Darren, who would end up being the main supplier to the whole *James' Home Services* network.

Darren taught me how to use his products and equipment and was always available for technical advice. He was a good guy and a huge help.

Secondly, I knew I needed to look professional, so I invested in a trailer, 500 brochures, uniforms, and business cards. I was off and running and looked the part to prove it. I had all the gear, but no idea what to do with any of it.

With that, I started my first ever marketing campaign. I took my 500 brochures and marched into all the local businesses. I was thinking, this won't be hard, I'll be flat out by next week.

Boy, I could not have been more wrong - again!

The problem was that I had no sales skills. And I mean—None. At all.

I was terrified as I walked into each business. I would literally throw my brochure on the front desk and run back out the door before they could say no, or anything else for that matter.

I got one $10 car wash out of those first 500 brochures; not quite what I had planned. Luckily, I finally realized that I was the problem. More importantly, I realized it was my lack of skills in this area that was the problem in both of my businesses.

I decided to learn: I found there were hundreds of sales books in the library and you could borrow them for free. So, I read ... and read ... and read. I tested the skills, measured the results, and wrote my own fool-proof rules.

I remember reading *The E-Myth* by Michael Gerber. I am not exaggerating when I say that this book completely changed my life. It taught me that long-term success in any business is all about the systems you put into place. I set about the systemisation of both of my businesses, and it changed everything!

My car cleaning business went through the roof. The systems were so good I could have had an 18-year-old run the business.

Our systems were very straight-forward, easy to follow, and very effective. I knew I had developed something special and that anyone who followed this recipe would have a very successful service business.

And with that ... the big dream was born.

I saw other service franchise systems and knew ours was better; because of the foundation that we had put into place. It quickly became clear that we had what it would take to build a large, successful network.

Then one fateful day, I was sharing this dream with a client and he was so impressed that he bought into the business immediately. Within two months we were selling franchises, and I was just 27 years old.

James' Home Services grew at a rapid rate. We quickly expanded throughout regional Queensland, and within two years we were the largest home services business in the state. The systems were created to stand the test of time and to grow with the business.

During this time, we not only grew the business, we also expanded into different services. Our services included car cleaning, house cleaning, external house cleaning, carpet cleaning, pest control, lawn and garden care, pet grooming, laundry and ironing services, as well as window cleaning.

The foundation we built transferred beautifully into each division of the business; just as it was designed to do. Our foundation was tested repeatedly, and never failed. Now, all we had to do was to develop the *technical* skills.

We went on to national expansion and eventually reached across Australia. We had a turnover of $20 million worth of services across the country each year.

After 20 years in the business, the network was sold to a commercial cleaning company.

In that 20 years, I saw thousands of families have successful home services businesses, with our proven systems at their core.

In this book, I am going to introduce you to my *Nine Foundation Steps*. These basic rules will show you step-by-step how to build an extraordinary home service business.

These rules will help you duplicate the foundation we built when we created *James' Home Services*.

The only catch is that you must use all of them if you want to be successful. Like all great recipes, they have to be followed rigorously if you want to get a consistent predictable outcome.

Chapter 1
Create Your Own Game

Running your own business is absolutely the best game in town. There is no other game that can give you as much fun, excitement, opportunities, and rewards that running your own business can give you. Running a successful business will change your life. However, many people get overwhelmed by the perceived pressure of the situation, allow stress to cloud their judgement, and make poorly thought-out decisions.

Just the thought that business is a *game* can totally freak many out. You may even argue that it is a battle to survive or a mountain that needs to be climbed. The fear of failure may be all that drives you to get up each day and face the battle ahead.

Survival Of The Fittest?

Don't get me wrong, it is vital that you survive financially in your business, because 89% of businesses do not survive the first 5 years. But it shouldn't just be about survival—it should be about having fun and enjoying (and I mean really enjoying) what you are doing.

The simplest way to guarantee the success of your business is to hit your targets as quickly as possible. This creates a fun game in your business and reduces your stress level dramatically.

How do you make your business a fun game instead of a battle for survival?

Every great game has a clear scoreboard. Quite simply—keep score.

All players need a clear picture of how they are performing— Are they leading the charge, bringing up the rear, or on the road to improvement? You must know where you stand at any given moment. Scoreboards motivate!

Keeping this in mind, the key is to build a series of scoreboards to measure your progress. These scoreboards will help you hit your key targets, and the visibility of your success will motivate you to reach for the next target or to deal with areas of your business that are underperforming.

Every professional player in every professional game knows the score. Not only do they know the overall score, but they know the *numbers on their own performance.*

The professional football player knows how many tackles they made, how many metres they ran, how many balls they dropped, and exactly how many tackles they missed.

The professional understands the final result is a reflection of these accumulation results. It is vital that a professional doesn't cheat the score. If you do so, you are only cheating yourself and the future of your business.

What Are Your Key Scoreboards?

Scoreboard #1—The Marketing

The Marketing is number one because it starts the momentum for everything else. The minimum marketing you have to do each day is 15 minutes. How you do this is up to you, but you must keep a record of the investment and the daily results.

Measure your marketing efforts in factual numbers. For example, my initial marketing consisted of driving to a suburb and delivering brochures in letterboxes and cold calling residents. Here's an example of what I measured:

Monday

- 10 Brochures dropped

- 5 Door knocks

- 1 Enquiry received

Wednesday

- 12 Brochures dropped

- 8 Door knocks

- 2 Enquiries Received

And so on throughout the week. Track each day, the activities and the results - every day. And I mean every day. Measuring activity helped me to quickly see patterns such as the best times/days to distribute my brochures. And that enabled me to react to those patterns as needed.

Scoreboard #2—The Sales Numbers

A professional service provider has to be a professional sales-person. Again, track every result. Be honest, be accurate and be real. For example:

Monday

- 2 Enquiries received
- 1 Face-to-face quote given/scheduled
- 1 New job booked in
- 2 Regular weekly clients booked in

Wednesday

- 3 Enquiries received
- 3 Face-to-face quotes given/=scheduled
- 2 New jobs booked in
- 1 Regular weekly client booked in

Again, and I cannot stress it enough—regular, detailed tracking of your activities and your results are only going to help you. The more detail you keep track of the quicker you improve your game.

Scoreboard #3—Your Client Base

The key target scores for servicing clients must be constant with your own goals. It is vital to keep your pre-set targets as a blueprint to the business you want to build. Your key measurements should be tracked both daily and weekly.

Think of it this way – if you need 30 clients per week break it down to six per day.

Then – if one day you are short you can make it a point to get it made up the next day. This will also help you see where you need to add new clients.

It is equally important to measure how often your clients are being serviced. Frequently, service business owners will decide that all their clients want their service done every two weeks, so that is what they recommend to all their clients, instead of asking what the individual clients want. Each client has different needs and you need to take this into account. Ask them what they want …

I recall coaching, Natalie, a very successful *James' Pet Grooming* franchisee. Natalie had a great business with over 200 grooming clients. She had a beautiful attitude and loved her business and every one of her four-legged clients truly loved her. She supplied an amazing level of service.

There was one thing that stood out with Natalie's *business scorecard.* She had a lot of clients. In fact, it was nearly twice as many as any other franchisee in our network, but she did not have twice the turnover as you might expect.

The *key score? All of her clients were booked in every four weeks.* Every single client—big dogs, small dogs, dogs living in units, dogs living on acreage, inside dogs, outside dogs, clean dogs, or dirty dogs.

In fact, she would *only* book her dogs in every four weeks—even when the dog-owner asked for more often. She had a very strong opinion in this area and truly believed doing it any more often was over-kill. No matter what argument we supplied she would not offer any service. Period. Other than four weeks.

Then after two years into her business, we started a new franchisee, named Catherine, in a neighbouring suburb. Amazingly, Catherine's business grew faster than Natalie's ever did. Her income had caught up to Natalie at the six-month mark.

How could this *newbie* franchisee fast track to the level of a long-term excellent performing franchisee in such a short time?

It was very simple actually.

Catherine had only 100 clients, but they were all every two weeks. Natalie had 200 clients but would ONLY service then every four weeks.

Catherine was delivering her service twice as often to half as many clients.

Customer Complaints Matter Too

Even dealing with your customer complaints can become a valuable scorecard. If you keep careful track of:

- All the complaints you receive from your clients.

- What were the issue or concerns they had?

- Any clients who cancel your services.

- Why did they cancel an appointment?

This information is very important to help you see possible customer service or communication issues within your business. A pattern of complaints can lead you to key areas of improvement in your business either within your systems or staff performance.

Keep score and don't let your opinions get in the way of the opportunities that can be in front of you. A third party can be so helpful as a sounding board. It is important to understand that a top coach or mentor who knows more about the game than you do can empower you to go to the next level and may even show you opportunities where you were too close to the action to see.

I personally have had either coaches or mentors all my working life. I believe it is important to surround yourself with people whom you can learn from.

The Gold

- Running your own business is the best game in town.

- The simple way to guarantee the success of your business is to hit the targets as quickly as possible, which creates a fun game in your business.

- Every great game has a clear scoreboard. Quite simply keep score.

- The key target scores for servicing clients must be constant with your own goals.

- Keep score and don't let your opinions get in the way of the opportunities that may be right in front of you.

- The professional understands the final result is a reflection of these constant results.

- It is vital that as a professional you don't cheat the score, you are only cheating yourself and the future of your business.

Chapter 2
The 9 Foundation Steps

The *James Home Services* network grew from my single business to a 400-franchisee strong group, servicing over $20 million in home services each year. We educated over 2,000 individual franchisees to build their own extraordinary service business under the *James* trademark for nearly 20 years.

But how did we do that?

We came up with a carefully thought-out system that could support our growth and then built our business on top of the foundation we created.

We have broken this system down into nine simple, easy to follow *Foundation Steps* that will ensure the success of your business - *if you follow them.*

These *Foundation Steps* have stood the test of time—and have worked nationally as well as internationally. Our franchisees were from many different nationalities and backgrounds and yet, the steps have consistently worked where it counts, in the actual marketplace.

Franchisee's paid considerable initial and ongoing fees to have access to these foundation steps because they consistently returned on the investment many, many times over. For those who choose to use them, these nine *Foundation Steps* will create extraordinary home service businesses.

I have added an extra foundation step for building your own brand. Under a franchise model, the branding step is done by the franchisor. I was that franchisor for all those years and we led the way in expanding the home service industry through franchising.

When I first started, the low entry-level franchise was a relatively new concept. Franchising was the best way to teach the average person how to run a great home-based service business.

I have always been a true believer in the free-enterprise system. There is nothing more rewarding than knowing you built your own business from concept into an extraordinary business success. I helped thousands of families to do just that.

I believe with the changes in technology we can now share these foundation steps with a greater market worldwide. We can help more families grow extraordinary businesses in more services and in more countries. If followed correctly, I know these important steps can take any business to an extraordinary level in a relatively short amount of time.

The 9 Secrets
To Extraordinary
Service Business Success

#1—Design Your Brand

This is where a franchisee network has a head start on the independent operator. The franchisor already has a brand and that brand should be well-known with credibility in the marketplace. But you can easily design your own *Local*

Professional Brand. With the use of the internet you have access to graphic artists and designers around the world who can help make your idea into your own professional brand.

You can build your own professional brand.

#2—Market Your Business Every Day

Marketing your business every day is just as much about the attitude as it is about the actions. It is about creating a habit of planting the marketing seed today to harvest the return in the future. Constant marketing activity will return a constant return in the long run. The key is to make this the most important step for today and the return will be there in the future.

How to market daily can take on many forms. We will take on both new age internet marketing to *old school* marketing. The rules to successful marketing haven't changed, just the medium we use to deliver it.

The how-to market is now more easily available to the average family home-based business.

#3—Get The First Job

There is no point in having a great looking brand and constant marketing if you don't have the quoting and sales process to convert the first enquiry. There is a definite process to get a high conversion rate with quoting on any services.

These quoting and sales processes will give you a 91% conversion rate in your face-to-face quotes.

These systems have been successful in more than eight different service business models. It is a matter of adopting the processes to your services, but the rules of presenting a successful quote will guarantee you get that vital *First Job.*

If you don't convert the initial quote, you can't get the long-term ongoing business. The ONLY way to build a regular client base is to Get the First Job.

#4—Always Deliver On Your Promises

If you promise something, then you should deliver it—*always*. This may sound rather simple, but many businesses make promises yet, they don't deliver.

If you promise *prompt, professional, and friendly services* you must deliver. Get to your client fast, be professional (on all levels), and be friendly. You will be stunned by how quickly your business will grow if you simply do what you say you will do.

Turning up when you say you will gives you a huge advantage over 90% of the service providers in the market. Most services providers simply don't show up when they say they will.

Turning up and delivering on your promises goes a long way towards being successful.

#5—Organise Your Business

This is the area where many good service businesses don't pay enough attention. You could be the greatest home cleaner, gardener, pet groomer, carpet cleaner, or computer programmer; but if you are so disorganised that you don't send invoices, pay your taxes, or do your follow-up marketing, your business will not get off the ground.

Area's concerning administration may be better off outsourced; doing so also requires some careful planning.

#6—Follow-up With Your Clients

Build a long-term relationship with your clients. Following up with them shows your clients just how much you value the relationship. By proactively asking the question you will be able to deal with any problems or areas of concern your clients may have.

The follow-up contact will also give you the opportunity to offer regular or additional services they are not currently taking advantage of.

#7—Continue To Deliver

It is one thing to turn up once and deliver on your promise. The real challenge is to always turn up and always deliver. Especially as you grow, and your business starts to take off, the pressure of success can test the systems that deliver your services.

If the client starts to feel neglected, or that your service standards have dropped, they will go looking elsewhere.

You will lose regular client if they perceive indifference on your part.

#8—Ask For The Referral

This is the fast track step that most service businesses simply do not do. If you are delivering the first seven steps, asking for the referral will send your business into hyperdrive.

#9—Repeat The Process

The ability to repeat the process over and over again, with every client, is the sign of a true professional. It takes true commitment to repeat this process. Sticking to your systems and building true foundations with a long-term commitment will give you an extraordinary home service business.

The Gold

- These foundation steps can take any business to an extraordinary level.

- You can build your own *professional brand*.

- Marketing your business daily is about an attitude as much as it is the actions.

- Turning up and delivering on your promise goes a long way to being successful.

- Many of the administration areas may be better off outsourced.

- If the client starts to feel neglected, or that your service standards have dropped, they will go looking elsewhere.

- Ask for referrals.

- Repeating the process is the sign of a true professional.

Chapter 3
You Have Decided You Want To Start Your Own Business, Now What?

You want to be your own boss; you are sick of working for someone else and just barely getting by; you get paid the same every week no matter how hard you work. Or maybe you fear that you could lose your job at any time? Perhaps you feel like it's time to make a change and take control of your future.

There is one major problem: you don't have a lot of money to invest in a business. You are in a position where you need to get a positive income quickly. You do have to feed yourself and/or your family, there are bills to pay each week, and you just can't wait months to get money coming in the door.

Is A Service Business Franchise Right For You?

So, you believe a *service* business is the best match for you and your family—it's relatively low-risk and offers positive cash flow reasonably quickly.

And with that, you decide to investigate the service franchise systems that are available in your marketplace. Many have proven systems, are well-known brand names, and have been around for over 25 years. They certainly should be able to fast track the growth of your business.

They should have the ability to market your business, grow your customer base, and even educate you on how to be a successful business owner.

Their systems have stood the test of time and you should be able to take advantage of that.

In most cases, the franchisors know what it takes to make your business work and, just as importantly, what will make your business fail.

A good franchisor has years of experience in their business, great documented systems, a proven record as a franchisor, a strong support structure, and solid plans for future growth. Becoming a franchisee in one of these networks may be a perfect fit for you.

The Only Problem Is ...

There is still one very big problem: you will need between $25,000 and $50,000 to invest in a quality system.

Some franchisors offer what's called *vendor financing*. This is when the franchisor loans the business owner the money to purchase into their franchise. These are a very dangerous trap for franchisees. You can find yourself relying on the franchisor to supply you with work, while at the same time owing them huge repayments.

This is a recipe for disaster and I recommend steering clear of these situations.

The ideal situation would be the best of both worlds:

- Have access to the knowledge and systems of the proven franchise network.
- The freedom of the independent service business.

That is exactly this book can give you. You can learn the trade secrets of a national service franchise directly from the founder of *James Home Services*.

I personally turned my one-man band car cleaning business into a national network of over 400 franchisees.

We were servicing approximately $20 million in home services each year. That is a lot of clean houses, mowed lawns, washed dogs, and detailed cars; and it all started with just one car client.

Over the course of 20 years, we helped more than 2000 families launch and sustain successful home service businesses. Our franchisees operated across many different services. These secrets have a proven track record that is second to none. If you follow these steps and develop them to suit your *service of choice* they will work.

What Do You Really Want?

The next challenge is deciding what you really want from your business. This can be very difficult at this stage and may seem too tough to answer because of all the uncertainty that surrounds the possible outcomes of your new venture. Believe me, I get it!

When we started a new franchisee, this was one of the first coaching questions we would ask. Understandably, many found this goal setting quite difficult. If setting specific goals is a new experience it can be quite unnerving.

But, it is vital to the success of your business no matter the field.

> *"You get what you plan to get. If you plan nothing then that is what you will get - nothing."*
>
> **Robert James**

I recommend you look at this on three levels:

1. The Long-term final finished business goals (5 to 10 years).

2. The Mid-range goals (1 to 2 years).

3. The NOW goals (1 month to 1 year).

The Long-Term Plan

What does your long-term, final, finished business look like? In the *big* picture give yourself the opportunity to dream big. Given the time and motivation, these principles will take your business to any level you choose.

I should also say that these are your goals and it is totally up to you what you want your business to look like. It doesn't matter if you plan to build a national home services network or a weekend business that can help fund your semi-retirement.

Document your personal goals and the business goals. Address your financial targets as well as your personal targets.

The Mid-Range Plan

These goals are the signs that you are heading in the right direction. These may be your first *reward* goals.

Perhaps a holiday you've always dreamed of, a new car, or the deposit for your new home. They might be business growth goals such as new employees, or personal goals like picking up your kids from school every day.

Give yourself clear targets and outcomes so you know when you have hit the mark.

The NOW Plan

What do you have to do right now? This plan is all about survival. If you don't survive until the 12-month mark, everything else is irrelevant. It is very true that you must have money to pay the bills, feed yourself, and to just get by.

We are starting this business understanding that you are on a limited budget and need a positive income quickly. You do need a *NOW Plan* and you need it right now.

The *Now Plan* may not be as inspiring as the *Mid-Range* and *Finished Business* goals. But they can be even more motivating. The fear of failure can certainly give you motivation to get yourself going.

The first thing you need in your *NOW Plan* is your break-even point. How much income do you need to be in a neutral cash flow position? How much turnover will be needed so you can hold your current position?

Reaching the break-even point as quickly as possible is vital. That will give you the time needed to develop your business and your own skill.

If You Survive You Can Learn To Thrive

The principles you will learn in this book will give you the tools to build an extraordinary home services business. Take the first step and decide what you want from your business. Everyone has different goals and will design their own interpretation of the home service business model.

Every one of our 400 franchisees had exactly the same business system that we helped put in place. But, each one built a different business that reflected their own personal needs and achievements.

The Gold

- A service business is a great business to start if don't have a lot of money to invest in a business. You need to get a positive income quickly.

- You can learn the trade secrets of a national service franchise directly from the founder of *James Home Services*.

- Decide what you really want from your business.

- You get what you plan to get. If you plan nothing then that is what your will get - nothing.

- If you survive you can learn to thrive.

Chapter 4
Which Service Should I Do?

Which Service Should I Do?

I must have been asked this exact same question at least a thousand times over the last 25 years. In the *James Home Services* network, we developed the systems for six different services businesses.

Our potential franchisees could choose which service best suited them and their family.

This decision had to be made before they became a franchisee; it's a very personal decision.

Throughout the recruitment process, this key factor was heavily focused on. Most potential franchisees came into our program thinking they knew what service they wanted to provide. However, nearly 50% of them changed their selection once they really understood the ins and outs of each business.

This process also gave them the opportunity to gain clarification on exactly what they wanted from their business, and what they really wanted to do.

What Do You Think?

The first question for you to ask yourself, and your partner if you have one:

What service business can I see myself doing?

For some of you this may be very clear. While others, not so much …

For example: If you love gardening and landscaping, do it with passion, and are good at it; running your own landscaping and gardening business may very well be your dream come true. You should chase that dream.

If you are a crazy dog or cat person who spends as much time as possible hanging with your four-legged friends, or if as a child you spent hours dreaming in the pet shop, then use your passion in a pet business such as grooming and hydro bath, dog walking, or pet minding.

If you are a true clean freak who gets the buzz out of cleaning the house from top to bottom, then you are a very valuable member of society. There are countless people who would love to pay you to show the same *enthusiasm* to keep their homes clean.

Are you a computer nerd who your friends call on to save their lost data or blue screen of death? You could be a true-blue handyman who can fix anything, anywhere, anytime, with the tools in the back of your ute. Maybe you're the car detailing freak who spends every Saturday morning cleaning your car until it is cleaner than the day it was brand new.

I think you get where I'm going with this—do you have a natural talent and love for something that is considered a service?

I would recommend starting there. If you love doing it for fun, imagine how much more you will love it when other people reward you for your enthusiasm and give you money to do it for them.

The funny thing is that if I had taken my own advice, I never would have started cleaning cars in the first place.

Before I started my car cleaning business, I certainly was NOT one of those people; I DID NOT love cleaning cars.

I was a horse trainer with young kids. My own car had always been very, very dirty.

The amount of hay, horse gear, and general rubbish I could gather in my car was scary. My family thought it was absolutely hilarious that I decided to start a car cleaning business. But I had good reason.

I started my original cleaning car service business because:

1.   It was a service that I could see myself doing.

2.   I believed other people would happily pay me to do it for them.

3.   The business was congruent with my family goals.

Does Your Service Of *Choice* Tick These Three Boxes For You?

Whether you have already decided on or you are still working out which service best suits you, I recommend you educate yourself on the opportunities in the market place. This simple, 5-step process before making a final decision.

A *Simple Business Plan*—Don't get carried away, just answer some simple questions:

1.   What do you want to achieve out of your business?

2.   How much do you need to earn to break-even?

3.   What are your first quarter income targets?

4.   What are your 12-month income targets?

5.   What about after that, long-term?

6.   Who is going to work in the business?

7.   List your practical strengths and weaknesses.

8.   What are your short-term and long-term family goals?

Do Your Homework—Take a good look around, where do you see a need or want for a service?

1. Investigate what services are happening in the major franchise networks. Generally, they do their homework—if a service has a strong demand, then there will likely be a major network already doing it. I would recommend you make an internet enquiry and investigate any service that jumps out at you.

2. Investigate local businesses. Look in your mailbox for brochures or the local papers or web pages. If there is already a business running the service in your area, then there is a demand for it. It is better to have competition than no demand. For example, you want to clean pools, but your immediate area has a very small percentage of built-in pools. Can you widen your service area or consider a different service?

Get Your Hands Dirty

Simply put, have a serious go at the services you are considering.

1. Spend a couple of days mowing your friends' lawns or cleaning their houses. You will certainly get a feel for what it is like to go into someone else's home and provide them with that service.

2. Go through the *recruitment* process with a franchise system. Many service franchise systems give a *day in the field* with one of their operators. Take the day and learn what they are doing well, what they are not doing so well. Getting your hands dirty is a great way to help you decide if that service really is for you.

3. Approach a potential supplier of products. A chemical supplier for example if you are considering cleaning. They may have current clients that would be able to give you some work or even train you (for a price of course).

4. Use a service provider and chat to them about their business.

Which Service Will Best Help You Reach Your Goals?

Write down the lessons you've learned; the pros and cons.

1. Is this a service that you can see yourself doing?

2. Do you believe other people would happily pay you to do the service?

3. Is this *service* business congruent with your personal goals and those of your family?

The Gold

- Even if you are set on one particular service, go through the steps with two different choices. You never know what the outcome will be, it might even change your mind.

- This process should clarify your own thinking. In favour or against your service choice.

- You will learn a lot about your industry very quickly.

- This education will become a part of the foundations that you build your business on.

Chapter 5
Design Your Own Brand

Do You Need A Brand?

You have decided to start your own business or may have already done so. However, you likely have no idea how to make it look like a professional brand.

Maybe you are not even convinced that you need to brand your business?

Many service providers get so caught up with doing the *work* that they think it is all that matters to their clients.

You may honestly believe it is all about mowing lawns, cleaning houses, washing dogs, fixing computers, or delivering coffee.

It's not ...

It is true that you must constantly deliver your service to keep your clients coming back. But—first, you must get the clients; beat out the competition, if you will.

So yes ... you DO need a brand! And ...

You Only Have One Chance ...

... to make a good first impression. I know we've all heard this many, many times. It is just as true in the small business world as it is anywhere else; perhaps even more so.

Many small, family businesses ignore the need to make the BEST first impression to get in front of a potential new client to give a quote, much less earn their business.

The Pro Marketer however, knows it is all about the first impression. That is how you get the client to contact you to begin with. *When there are other people providing the same service, how do you stand out?* In the beginning, it doesn't matter who provides a better service, it's about who is better at getting their attention.

This is one of the biggest advantages the franchise networks have on the independent operator. In most franchise networks, the branding is professional and reflects a professional service that a client expects.

If your branding promises professional friendly service, then the client expects professional and friendly. If your branding looks amateur or cheap, or worse, looks like you couldn't even bother to try—what message are you sending? If you were a potential new client, looking for the service you are providing, would you call you?

So, how can you as an independent small business owner create the image that will position you favourably against the larger, more well-known brands? It is vital that you invest in the branding of your business from day one. Each day you then reinforce the brand in your marketplace.

If you can believe it, it takes anywhere from three to six exposures to your brand for the average person to recall it. And do not worry about overexposure—there is no such thing.

The investment in your branding is as vital as the equipment you need to run your business. You can't run a successful dog washing business without a dog bath or without professional branding.

How do you decide what it should look like? Where do you start?

I've Outlined Some Simple, Proven Steps To Get You Going

1. Choose a Clear, Descriptive Name That Attracts Your Target Clients

At *James Home Services* we were a *Home Services* business, not just a cleaning business; offering a wide range of home services. If you want home services done just call *James.*

The image of the professional friendly butler in his formal refined tuxedo then connected to *James Home Services* which became part of the customer's collective subconscious.

The business name should say what you do. It should be what your clients would search for when they are looking for your services.

If you are a *commercial cleaning business* be sure to make that very clear. If you claim to be a *home cleaning business* and chase both markets, it can be very confusing. Marketing towards home clients is very different than marketing to commercial cleaning clients. Make up your mind in the beginning and name your business that way.

Be creative with your name and make it easy to remember. If you work in a particular geographical area it is fine to put that in your name. That can be an advantage to gaining local clients but could work against you if you plan to expand to a wider territory.

As an example, *Mooloolaba Home Cleaning Services* is perfect if you plan to build your business of cleaning homes in Mooloolaba. It is nearly the perfect word search for your business.

Sea Breeze Home Services is perfect for a coastal home services market.

Ninja Computer Solutions is great for the guy who can fix those annoying computer issues. Everyone ends their personal *Computer Ninja* who can just turn up and take down those computer demons.

2. Decide On *The Look* You Want For Your Business.

Take the time to brainstorm on this one.

- What is the overall style that you are after?
- The colours, the feel, and the image?
- Are you going for an upscale, mid-range, or lower-end image?

This will likely depend on your target market. It is a *look* that you personally can take ownership of. It is the logo that will be on your uniforms, business cards, website, and all of your signage. Be sure you love it as you are going to have to live with it—hopefully, for a very long time.

The *look* should be relatable to your target clients. If you are marketing to the top-end market, then design a top-end look.

Use colours and images that reflect the premium market you are aiming for. Once you decide on *The Look*, it is vital to be consistent in all your marketing.

3. A Professional Logo Is A Big Advantage

Create a clever *logo* for your business. The Logo image is what will stick in the minds of your clients. Think about all the businesses that come to mind, you will likely remember the image as the business. It is very hard to even imagine *McDonalds* without thinking of the *Golden Arches*, don't you think?

Your logo should flow into your business name. We were *James Home Services* and the image of *James* the *friendly butler* clearly flows with it.

If you're anything like me, you probably can't draw.

I'm about to give you a *Family Business Life Hack*. It is called *Upwork*. I absolutely love *Upwork* (*www.upwork.com*). With *Upwork* you can hire professionals from all around the world to get your idea transformed into reality. No matter your need, you can find help on *Upwork*.

4. A *Tagline* That Tells The Story

At *James Home Services* our first tagline was, *Prompt, Professional, Friendly Service*. It told our story, it was exactly what we offered and exactly what our clients expected.

As we grew, and our marketing evolved, we positioned ourselves directly against our main competitors. Our service was more upmarket. We invested in a professional spokesperson, champion swimmer Tracey Wickham (Olympian, World Record holder and Commonwealth Games gold medalist).

We evolved our tagline to *Gold Medal Service* which served us for over 15 years. Over the years, our spokesperson changed to Steven Bradbury, the last man standing speed skater, (Winter

Olympian and Australians first winter Olympics gold medalist); but our tag line stayed the same—it continued to tell our story.

Tell your own story with your tag line.

5. Feedback From Focus Groups

If you have doubts about the images for your business, ask a group of your target market the questions—a focus group. Always give the possible alternatives and get them to rate them from best to worst. And then, be sure to invest the time to get very clear on what your business will look like when it is done.

Most family-run business don't do these steps.

Many larger organisations even attempt to ignore these marketing realities. The business owner must have a clear, consistent look for their business. If there is no clarity, then the client will get confused and go elsewhere. Built to a professional standard and correctly implemented, your brand will become the most valuable intellectual property asset that you ever own.

You only get one chance to make a good first impression. A professional business owner makes it count!

The Gold

- Your business needs a *brand*.

- Most family businesses fall into the trap of ignoring the necessity of making the BEST first impression.

- Be creative with your name and make it easy to remember.

- Decide on *the look* you want for your business.

- Create a clever *logo*. The logo image is what will stick in the minds of your clients.

- Tell your story in your tag line.

Chapter 6
Market Your Business Every Day
It's All About An Attitude

Marketing your business every day is all about an attitude. You plant your marketing seeds today for a future harvest of business income. The marketing you do today will come back in the future. The marketing you don't do today will reap nothing—you will only reap what you sow.

I learned this very important concept very early in my business career. I was a horse trainer struggling to make ends meet. As a 23-year-old father of two young kids I decided that a part-time car cleaning business would be a great way to help feed my young family.

We All Have A First Time

My first marketing campaign was 500 two-colour brochures and me. I figured that if I just walked into local businesses they would be jumping all over me to get their dirty vehicles cleaned.

How hard would it be? I knew I'd easily get about 100 clients from my 500 brochures.

I could not have been more wrong. Well—I only got one $10 car wash. Yes, your read that right—just one car to clean in 500 businesses.

Learn From Your Mistakes

I think it takes a smart business-person to be able to step back a bit and gain perspective. It helps to see what the issues in the business might really be.

I did realise that I may have been the issue. I reviewed my *script* or lack thereof, read and learned as much as I could about sales, got 500 more brochures printed, and headed back to the same 500 businesses.

I didn't get through to all of the business but, I did do surprisingly well. The second time around I got about $1,000 in work. I was off and running! It took me about a week to get all the cars washed and done, and then I was back in the same position—I had no work again.

Off I went in a panic and did another marketing campaign. I got about the same results – $1,000 worth of business from 500 brochures.

This up and down pattern went on for about 6 months. I would have one great week followed by a slow week; then another great week followed by another slow week. You can probably see where I'm going with this but ... at the time the inconsistency in my turnover was making me crazy. I could not figure out why every second week was a *bad* week.

I sat down and took a hard look at exactly where my clients were coming from and realized that they were all being pulled in from my marketing campaigns.

No one was just turning up on my doorstep begging me to wash their cars. Each wave of clients came in when I was marketing and I was only marketing when I wasn't cleaning cars. Do you see the mistake I was making?

Hence the up and down business—I wasn't marketing every day. If I was too busy cleaning cars, I wouldn't bother with my marketing.

And that's when it occurred to me—if I wanted consistent business I needed consistent marketing efforts. Even if I was busy cleaning cars I needed to market every single day for the future business.

You Are Never Too Busy To Be Marketing Your Business

Marketing had to be the most important task of the day. The marketing I did each day secured future business. I set a new rule—I did not go home until I had invested 15 minutes each day into marketing for future clients. This was one of the best business decisions I've ever made.

The business began growing more consistently. Little by little, new clients *magically* appeared every day. Some came from marketing I did 6 months earlier, others from the marketing I did just yesterday. Marketing daily worked, and it was as much about an attitude change as the action itself. The cause and effect were very clear.

Plant the marketing seeds and your business will bloom.

I had business coming in consistently, the ups and downs had flattened out, and the turnover began growing consistently every week. The profitability and goodwill in my business was growing with it as well.

I found I was working less but making more money.

Finally, the work seemed to be coming to me. I had created an effective business model by investing 15 minutes each day into marketing for the future. 15 minutes every day will make a successful business?

As the years pasted, and I expanded into franchising *James Home Services*, this key rule was the cornerstone to our rapid growth. Every single one of the *James Home Services* franchisees were taught to market their business every day. It was a cultural expectation for every franchisee in the network.

We empowered our franchisees to take control of their own business growth. We trained our people on how to market effectively, we gave them the marketing tools and support that was needed. Only 15 minutes every day and their business would bloom.

How Does It Work?

You may be asking yourself, how do I market every day? How do I market when I am so busy I can barely catch my breath?

You do it because you have to do it. There are many different ways to market a business. Where do you start?   Here are the things all start-up businesses must have:

- **A Good Brochure:** Full colour, foldout with a complete menu of your services and a starting price. You should always have a *From $55* price, a *From $35* price or whatever your lowest price point may be. This helps your potential customers realize you're not too expensive for them.
  You also need direct contact details on the back.
  Drop at least ten brochures every single day.

- **Professional uniform:** This should be in your *corporate colours.* Collared shirt with logo visible on the chest. You should never be in front of a client without a uniform. Like *Superman* you are only *Clark Kent* without the right outfit. Keep a clean shirt in your vehicle for quoting ONLY. Wearing a uniform that is clean and in good repair will always enhance and maintain your professional appearance.

- **Professional Signage:** The investment in signage on your vehicle is key. Whether you use a van, car, or a trailer, sign it up professionally in your brand. The amount of walk up clients because of the signs will pay back 100-fold over the years. Not having professional signage will actually damage your credibility. If you turn up in an unmarked vehicle, you will lose work to the professional who arrives in the fully signed rig.

- **Business Facebook Page:** This can be put together very cost effectively; targeted towards the clients in your geographical service area. Then post to promote the services you have to offer. Engage happy clients whenever you can. People love to read positive reviews so encourage your happy clients to like you on *Facebook*. It builds creditability faster than you realize.

- **Professional Website:** This doesn't have to be complex. A simple, three to four page website can do the trick. These days, without a website you will have no credibility with your clients. But keep it simple and use plenty of images.

The Do's And Don'ts

Every time you interact with a client, you are the marketing and sales manager of your business. Keep this in mind every time you speak with someone.

Clients are expecting you to behave and present yourself and your business with high professional standards. I've put together a list of *Do's* and *Don'ts* that you should always keep in mind when you are interacting with customers.

DO

- DO smile

- DO say *please* and *thank you*

- DO show interest when they are talking

- DO give your client the chance to speak

- DO listen

- DO stand upright and confident

- DO be relaxed

- DO project your voice

- DO ask if they want the job done now

DON'T

- DON'T have a bad attitude

- DON'T frown or whinge

- DON'T speak softly

- DON'T hunch over

- DON'T be untidily dressed

- DON'T be disillusioned if you get *No's*. The *Yes* may come later, after you do your follow up procedures

- DON'T forget to follow up

Marketing your business daily is all about an attitude. Your actions must back up the attitude. I wouldn't go home until I did my 15 minutes of marketing every day. I know it can be hard sometimes, but you must make the decision to do it and stick with it. It will pay for itself many times over!

I remember one day in particular. It was a couple of days before Christmas and I'd had a record day: I had made about $700 for the day, a huge figure 25 years ago. I was heading home, I was exhausted, and was quite pleased with my days' work. But I had one problem: I was too busy to market this day.

I was nearly home, and I found I was making excuses for myself, "Don't worry about it."

But I know what I should do, so I stopped the car, grabbed 20 brochures and ran up the street and dropped them in random mailboxes. I felt better and was able to go home and enjoy dinner with my family without worry. And honestly, I thought I wouldn't get anything from that brochure drop.

Early the next morning though, magically, I got a call for an urgent car detail from the brochures I had dropped the night before. It shows you, even a few extra minutes pays off two-fold!

When *Marketing Your Business Daily* becomes a habit, success will also become a habit. Plant the marketing seeds and your business will bloom.

The Gold

- *Market Your Business Daily* is all about an attitude. You plant your marketing seeds today for a future harvest of the business income.

- The wave of clients always came after I would market.

- Marketing then became the most important task of the day. I didn't go home until I had invested 15 minutes each day into marketing for tomorrows clients.

- The payoff for my business was very clear. I had a consistent turnover.

- I expanded into franchising *James Home Services*, this key rule was the cornerstone to our rapid growth.

- *Market Your Business Daily* was a cultural expectation for every franchisee in the network.

- How do you market daily? Must haves: uniform, brochures, signage, *Facebook* page, website, and your attitude.

- *Market Your Business Daily* is about an attitude. Your actions must back up the attitude.

Chapter 7
Your Target Market

One of the biggest challenges in the early days of your business will be getting new clients. You will be so keen to get new clients that you will chase any work, anywhere, at any price, and at any time. It is understandable, you have bills to pay and you are feeling uncertain about your new businesses venture.

How FAR Should You Go?

My business was just starting to take off after I'd had a very slow start. At this stage, I had a wife and two young sons to feed. I was still very desperate to make an income.

I got a call for a partial car detail in Noosa, which was about 40 minutes outside of my regular client area. I decided to take the booking for four o'clock on Friday afternoon.

Of course, when Friday arrived business was booming. Everywhere we stopped we were picking up more and more work. The cash was flowing, my offsider and myself were working like a well-oiled machine. Business was going great.

Then, it got to be three in the afternoon, I have people in front of me that want their cars cleaned, right now.

But—I also have a commitment to drive the 40-minutes to Noosa to make the appointment that I had booked earlier in the week. I say *no* to the clients standing in front of me and start the drive.

I was not a happy car cleaner—cursing myself the entire drive. *What was I thinking? Why take a job so far away in a prime time of my week?* There I am sitting in traffic, paying my offsider to sit in the car with me for the 40 minutes to the job, and then paying him to go back home. I even had to stop to fuel up.

I got to the client's home and cleaned their car like a true professional, knowing I was doing the job for nothing. I could have made more money if I just stayed on my home turf for the day. I learnt a very valuable lesson that day that I taught to many franchisees for the next 25 years.

"He who chases two rabbits, catches neither."

Confucius

You Have To Make A Choice

The same goes for any service business. Decide on your client and chase them. Running after everyone gets you nothing.

For example: if you are a cleaning business, you have three different clear client markets:

1. Commercial Cleaning

2. Move Out or Bond Cleaning

3. Regular, Domestic Cleaning

These are three very different clients and decision makers. Different clients require very different services. They *value* the services differently.

In commercial cleaning the *service* is bought as a product. Mostly under a tender agreement, that is decided as a *necessity*. The goal of the manager in charge is to get the cheapest price for the service. This market is very price driven.

In the *Move Out* or *Deposit/Bond Cleaning* market the decision maker is the Property Manager even though they don't actually pay for the services. Their goal is to get the tenant to pay to clean the property to a standard that it is rentable again. They can be very picky and will expect you to revisit the property; and the tenant will have to pay for your time.

The regular, domestic home client wants professional, friendly and prompt service. They want to be able to trust you to be inside their home when they are not at home. They want a service provider who delivers professional service, is a good communicator, and delivers the service as promised. They will pay a premium for excellent service and build a long-term relationship with a service provider they can trust.

The marketing here is very different as well, as we shall discuss later. Your marketing should reflect the different decision makers and the most effective ways to reach each of them.

Every service has different possible client bases. You should choose the client base that best suits the goals of your business; taking your own personal skills, strengths, and weaknesses into consideration.

One of the key components for many service providers is frequency of the return client. If you have a business based on regular, weekly services you can get by with fewer clients than a business which relies on annual return clients. The more often your clients return, the less of them you need ...

Geographically, Where Should You Get Your Clients From?

The simple answer is, as close to home as you can. In the service industry, you are selling your time, and the more you travel the less time you have to sell. The more you drive to service a client the more expense you will incur. The maintenance, fuel, and the wear and tear on your vehicles and yourself can kill you in the long run.

At *James Home Service*, I had a formula to get the most effective return for our franchisees. I took into consideration the franchisees geographical area, the return frequency of the service, as well as the average cost of the service.

Be Realistic

The more frequent the return client the smaller the area. Weekly to fortnightly only needed 40 clients to be *full*. A target area of 1000 homes was perfect. Generally speaking, services that have a long frequency, like window cleaning, have a higher average job price. It may take a full day to clean all the windows in your average house.

The window cleaning client returns roughly every three months. So, window cleaners need 65 to 80 clients to be considered "full." The target market area would be 4000 homes. And so on ...

If you spread yourself too thin you will get a diluted market coverage, costs will increase, and your time will be wasted on travel instead of paid services.

Give yourself a clear target for what your client base will look like. If there are dogs to wash on your street, why drive 30 minutes to a client on the other side of town? Build your clients to suit your diary and keep them close to each other. You will thank yourself when you are not spending hours of unproductive time behind the wheel.

In the beginning, you will be so keen to get any job that you will most likely drive anywhere. Sometimes this can be successful in the short-term but, understand that there will come a time when you will have to let the clients that are out of the way go to fit in more profitable clients.

Your final client base should be made up of clients who happily pay your required rate, are geographically in close to each other and a consistently regular return service.

This may sound a bit heartless but if it is a professional service business you are building then the outcome is to build the most efficient business possible.

The Gold

- You will be so keen to get new clients that you will be inclined to chase any work, anywhere, at any price—DON'T!

- "He who chases two rabbits, catches neither." Says Confucius

- Decide who your client is and chase them.
  Running after everyone gets you nothing.

- Different clients require very different services. They *value* the services very differently.

- One of the key considerations for many service providers is frequency of the return client.

- In the service industry, you are selling your time.
  The more you travel the less time you have to sell.

- If you spread yourself too thin you will get a diluted market coverage. Costs will increase, and your time will be wasted on travel instead of paid services.

Chapter 8
The Six Times Marketing Rule

The number SIX is the *magic number* in all aspects marketing.

On average, it takes about six contacts to get any real brand power happening at every level of your marketing. As such— your marketing goal is to repeat your brand message to your target clients at least six times.

The pattern of response from your market will increase with each marketing contact. Think of six as your magic number— no one will remember you until they have been *touched* by your marketing efforts at least six times.

Those six contacts do not have to be in the same medium. It's actually better if they are a mixture of mediums.

The client may see the signage on your vehicle, a brochure in the mailbox, your add on *Facebook*, the local paper adds, or an add on television. And, in this day and age, if you're lucky, they will see all of these.

Most small business owners give up before they get the traction in the marketing they really need to be successful. This is one of the biggest advantages of a franchise system: the ability to get the brand in clients' heads. They have a head start with their brand traction, but you can outperform the big brands if you understand the *Six Times Rule*.

Building Your Power Brand

Even if you are a small business, you can still build your own *Power Brand* if you follow the basic teachings of the *Six Times Rule*.

Clients are most comfortable with a brand they recognise. Familiarity comes from repetition. The more times clients see your message, the more likely they are to trust you.

A well-presented brand that is easy to remember and recognise is very helpful, but repetition can compensate for a *plain* brand image.

Reach And Frequency

The balance between *reach* and *frequency* is the key to really building your brand. *Reach* is the overall number of people that have seen your marketing, while *frequency* is how many times they have seen it.

Small business owners frequently make the mistake of trying to reach too many people at once.

A marketing campaign that reaches 6,000 people (reach) just once (frequency) will fail. Instead, you could use the same resources to market to 1000 people (reach) and repeat the campaign *Six* times (frequency) and you will get a much more effective use of your limited marketing resources.

You want to be the big fish in the small pond, not the other way around. Target a smaller market and take ownership of that market. You can beat a franchise brand if you challenge them on your terms.

Be the most famous lawn mower, house cleaner, dog groomer, car detailer, coffee van, or computer nerd in your market. Keep your target market smaller and keep repeating your brand message to *that* market.

Don't leave the door open for a competitor to get a foot in the door of your local market. You want to be the first service provider who comes to mind when anyone in your area wants your service. That can only come from repeating your message within your target market at least six times.

At *James Home Services*, our franchisees were all given enough brochures to cover their area the magic six times. If they had a protected suburb of 1000 homes, their start-up kit would have 6000 full colour brochures. This was on top of the heavy marketing we did on television, websites, radio, and on social media.

However, the top performers were the franchisees who excelled at using their brochures and tools repetitively. Franchisees that underperformed or failed in the *James Home Services* system would in the vast majority of occasions *refuse* to target market their own area. Relying on the franchisor's marketing always leads to underperformance.

When you start your service business it is vital you understand the power of the *Six Times Rule*.

From day one budget to market to your client base six times.

If you don't want to do this don't bother even starting. You will fail!

I will talk more about how to best use both *old school* and *new school* marketing tools a bit later. There are many effective tools available in the market these days that were not available to franchisees when I started out over 25 years ago. There are still many tools that have always worked and still do. But—more on this later …

How Fast Do You WANT To Grow?

The faster you get your frequency up to the magic six times, the faster your business momentum will take control. The more advertising you do within your target market, the more clients you will get, and the faster you will grow.

It's a bit like a restaurant that is full compared to one that is empty. More customers want to go to the busy restaurant believing that the group has chosen the one with the best food. Happy clients certainly bring more happy clients. The more you are seen working in your area, the more business you will get.

The Grass Is *Not* Always Greener

Do not fall for the grass is greener syndrome. I have seen countless numbers of services providers decide the *other area* is better than their own particular target area. It always reminded me of the horse leaning over the fence to get the greener grass outside of their paddock.

My 40-minute drive to Noosa and back confirmed the folly in this. They would market their area maybe once (if at all), then start randomly marketing other areas and wonder why they weren't getting an effective response.

If you spread your marketing and yourself too thin, you will never end up with a business that works for you. You end up working for nothing, that is if you end up getting any work at all.

Once you get your six times coverage in your target area— keep going! Unless you have all the business you can handle and that none of your clients will ever leave you? Likely not. Your potential clients are changing every day. They will use your services when they need them, not always when you want them to.

People's circumstances are constantly changing—they move, get new jobs, lose jobs, and have babies. Perhaps they have sudden health issues, or a new dog or cat joins their family, or a competitor tries to move in on them?

All those things and many more are changing in your target market every day. As a professional services provider, you are there to give the time back to your clients when they need you.

Always aim to be the brand that comes to mind first within your target market and you will be well on your way to having a professional, successful business.

The Gold

- The number six is the magic number in all marketing.

- Most small business owners give up before they get traction in their market.

- Balance between reach and frequency is the key.

- You want to be the big fish in the small pond. Target a smaller market and take ownership of that market.

- When you start your service business it is vital you understand the power of the six times rules.

- The faster you get your frequency up to the magic six times, the faster your businesses momentum will take control.

- Don't fall for the grass is greener syndrome.

- Be the brand that comes to mind first in your target market and you will be well on your way to having a professional, successful business.

Chapter 9
The DIY Marketing Plan

It seems as though many people think that marketing is some sort of black magic or you need to be an internet marketing guru to get a handle on it; only these gifted individuals can possibly successfully market a business, right?

Wrong. The reality is that you can market your own business if you use the tools available correctly and consistently. Most small businesses ignore the basic foundation tools for marketing their own business.

The first step is to have a plan and stick to it over a long enough period of time to get the results.

Remember, the six times rule applies to all marketing tools.

The key is to invest wisely, constantly, and consistently to get the reputation out there and to be easily recognised by your target market.

The Best Way To Start

I know what you're thinking—*there are so many tools to market my business, where do I start?* The answer is actually very simple—a combination of *New Age* tools and *Old School* techniques!

In any home service industry, it is important to remember that your market is still actually at home. Every house still has a mailbox, a front door, and the internet.

Keeping this in mind, I recommend a marketing plan that combines a bit of old school and new age marketing to get the best results. Create your plan and then stick to it.

Old School Marketing Is Still Very Cool

Uniforms

First impressions are vital. If you look like a professional, you are halfway there. Whereas, if you look like a hobo, then you have no chance of building trust with your clients. A professional uniform is vital to any services business.

The colours, and the look must be consistent with your modern image. You want to present as a professional service provider, not like a 1980's bowling team. Think sharp, neat, clean, modern, and tidy. No mismatches, like throwing on your favourite football team socks or cap just because you feel comfortable in them.

The uniform should always be worn by all team members and should be from head to toe. Consistent, professional look that parallels with the overall look for your business is the simple equation. Remember—stains and rips are not okay. All uniforms must be updated on a regular basis.

Full Colour Brochures

For the home service industry, these are a key marketing tool that many home-based businesses ignore. They work with a long lifespan in your client's homes.

The brochure should:

- Be in full colour
- Contain photos of you and your team doing the services you supply
- Include a full menu of all services offered

Brochures are an excellent way to source new work. On average, brochures will have a redemption rate of approximately 3% over time. This means that if you distribute 1000 brochures, you should get a return of at least 30 jobs from those brochures.

The colour brochures have a longer than usual shelf life.

At *James Home Services*, franchisees found that they received benefit from brochure drop-offs long after they distributed them.

With each job you do in your area you should drop at least five brochures on either side of your job location. By doing it this way, you make better use of your time dropping your brochures close to where you are as opposed to driving to a specific location just to drop off brochures.

When you start your business target your area by dropping your brochures in mailboxes.

- 1st week: 2500 brochures

- 2nd Week: 500 brochures

- 3rd Week: 500 brochures

- 4th Week: 500 brochures

- 5th Week: 500 brochures

Once you complete a job that came from your brochure drop, drop five brochures on either side of the home you just serviced. Alternatively, knock on the neighbour's door, let them know you are working next door, hand them your brochure, and ask if they could use your services.

Vehicle Signage

Professional signage is a must on all your vehicles. It even works when you're not working. Potential clients will see you everywhere—when you are working on their street, when you are doing your shopping, or dropping the kids off at school.

The signage encourages potential clients to contact you.

If your services use a trailer, great! It creates a great mobile billboard. With no signage, no real business, and it looks very untrustworthy.

Business Cards

These are an absolute must for any business—and I am NOT talking about the kind you print *really quick* on your own printer. Professional business cards are a great tool to use when you meet your clients face-to-face.

Colours that are consistent with your branding are very important. I recommend using the back of your card to list the services you offer. Clip them to your quotes as well, so they are simple, and easy to find if your client has questions.

Printed Branded Quote Book

The quote book will become a vital tool in your sales process—this is another must have. It should be consistent with your brand image, include your logo and contact details, printed on full A4-sized paper, and be very simple and professional in nature.

Think of making it easy to read, easy to understand, and making the decision to call you also very easy.

New Age Marketing Can Take You To New Heights

Small business owners these days have so many options to market their business on-line that it can easily seem confusing. Modern marketing rightfully revolves around the internet, but many businesses get pulled in so many different directions that it can be completely overwhelming.

I highly recommend keeping it SIMPLE.

Only target clients for your services within your specific target area.

There are simple, easy to navigate *New Age Tools* that work very effectively for home service businesses.

Professional Website

Invest in a site that you can be proud of. Keep in mind the main purpose is for it to be search friendly for *clients who need your services in your area*. This may sound scary but all it really means is that it should be built using content that is all about the needs and wants of your target market.

There are many online consultants that can do this for you at very competitive costs. *Upwork.com* is a great place to find experts from all around the world. You can cost-effectively build a professional website using your own content.

Business Facebook Page

Remember, the key is to build a page that is for clients in your area, who need your services. They call it *social media* for a reason—it is social, so be social. Use posts that engage your clients socially and post something interesting every day.

Facebook marketing can be a very cost-effective tool for the home services provider. Keep your target market tight, your area, your service is the simple answer.

Your Own Blog Page

Yes, be a blogger. Post a blog with content about your services. One post a week with local content and you will be the local expert in no time. When someone searches your service in your area you can be the go-to guy or girl at least. There are some great online training programs available to educate yourself in this area.

I know this may seem like a lot of information and it may

sound a bit overwhelming, but this is what every franchise network does. You can pay them up front, on an ongoing basis, or you can go the DIY route. It's up to you.

If you don't market at all, you will likely fail, and your business will become a chore. The opposite is also true—embrace the DIY marketing plan and grow your business to whatever goals you may have.

The Gold

- Marketing may seem like some sort of black magic or be an internet marketing guru to get a handle on it.

- The reality is that you can market your own business if you use the tools available correctly and consistently.

- The first step is to have a plan and stick to it over a long enough period of time to get the results from it.

- Old School Marketing is still very cool.

- New Age Marketing can take you to new heights.

- Embrace the DIY marketing plan and grow your business to whatever goals you may have.

Chapter 10
Professional Sales Systems

You can have the greatest branding ever, an awesome marketing campaign, and deliver the gold-medal level service every time, but if you don't get that first job, it is all adds up to nothing.

Poor, ineffective, or non-existent sales systems destroy businesses. The good news is that the opposite is also true—professional, effective, client-friendly, and efficient systems power businesses to the next level.

With The Right Systems You WILL Succeed

At *James Home Services*, our franchisees averaged a 91% close rate on first appointments, when they utilized these systems. These quoting or sales systems have stood the test of time; they have been systematically developed, taught, and used throughout the last 25 years.

Our carefully and methodically planned sales and quoting systems were our biggest advantage over our competitors. No one else put the time and energy into their systems that we did.

We tested and measured every aspect of our quoting systems. Simply put, we made sure they worked. And a franchisee that used our quoting system got the first job nine out of ten times. I am sure you can imagine the effect that level of conversion rate will have on your return on investment (ROI) of your marketing dollars.

Whether You Like It Or Not

A professional quoting or sales system is vital to long-term success in the service industry. Most services providers have neglected the *process* of the sale of their services. Some may even believe that quoting is not sales. Many service providers leave their sales to a random chance and their process varies from quote to quote, depending on how they feel today or at the whim of their various potential clients.

I believe first, we must talk about how many people who enter the services industry have a personal objection to selling their product. These limiting beliefs keep individuals and their companies from using excellent sales systems.

The Used Car Salesman Image

You may have been educated that a sales person is bad.

The image and belief that a salesperson is dishonest, lying, pushy, or even evil is a false stereotype. That is what a BAD salesperson is.

So, don't be that person, it just doesn't work. Be honest, upfront, friendly, confident, an effective communicator, and a caring leader. Plus, it works better in the long run anyway.

The second factor to talk about is the fear of rejection; no one enjoys hearing the word *No*.

No one wants to fail, and many will go a long way around to try and avoid the possibility of even getting close to the word *No*.

This is exactly why an established quoting and sales system is vital. If you get nine out of every ten quotes, you are certainly avoiding rejection by being a success. *Yes* is the best cure for rejection fears. But even more importantly, the *Sales Process* takes the perceived danger of rejection away from the business owner. The client is rejecting the quote … not the person.

A Very Important Tool

Use your sales and quoting systems as a tool as much as you use your mower, vacuum, or your hydropath. If you really don't want to sell your services, DON'T go into your own business. Every business has to sell, or it is not a business.

There are seven steps to an effective professional quoting system that commence after the marketing has done its job and the potential client calls you.

The Seven Steps To Effective Quoting System

- Step #1—Calling the Customer Back

- Step #2—Booking the Appointment

- Step #3—The Individual Quote

- Step #4—Education of Options

- Step #5—Closing the Quote

- Step #6—Handling Objections

- Step #7—Following up on the Quote

There are more details to follow on each of these steps. Each and every one of them is vital in the process. If you have a high-end service, you may need even more steps. They will be extensions of these basic steps and may be required to get more detailed information or build more trust. For example:

When we sold franchises at *James Home Services* it was a ten-step process. This is very understandable as we were asking a franchisee to invest their whole business future, and sometimes their life-savings in our product.

The franchise product was all based around marketing, support, and training services. It was a $30,000 product and the potential client needed time to understand what they were investing in.

A services quote is very straight-forward. The potential client wants or needs someone to help them. They want help with the things they either cannot do, do not want to do, or simply do not have the time to do. You are giving your client's their time back. This is not a hard concept to sell.

Everyone loves a great service provider, you just have make sure they know that you are the one for them from the very first meeting. The key is to make it easy for your client to use your service, you don't want to become the objection.

The Other Side Of The Table

I recently had the experience of getting a cleaning on my own home as a client. It was a strange feeling considering I had had my own cleaning business for 20 years. It was certainly an interesting experience being on the receiving end of the service.

I will say this, the couple who attended my home did turn up in uniform and with a beautifully signed vehicle. But from that point on their quoting process was very confusing and nearly non-existent.

The woman seemed friendly, the man? Not so much. They spent about 15 minutes wandering around the house and he complained a lot! He whined about the house being too big, the ceilings being too high, and the house needing at least a full day of work.

Whenever the woman would offer suggestions, he would immediately shut her down. He was obviously angry with her and very negative towards me.

He told me more than once how busy he was and that he didn't want to waste his time quoting if he wasn't going to get the job.

At the end, he came up with a quote of $550. The house would be cleaned top to bottom and they would do it in two days' time. This worked perfectly for my requirements and I thought the quote was reasonable. There was no written quote, even though I asked for one. He said there was no need for one, he always does what he says he is going to do.

I actually felt sorry for the woman. She did seem to be genuine and unfortunately for her, she was married to and in business with *Oscar the Grouch*. I think I gave them the job partly out of sympathy for the woman.

The day of the cleaning arrived, and to my pleasant surprise, started very early that morning at 6:30am. In came *Oscar the Crouch* and his sweetheart wife. Maybe I was wrong. Perhaps her attitude will be enough to get the work done?

Well, at about 10:30 everything imploded. *Oscar* the cranky franchisee pulled the biggest tantrum I have ever seen from a grown man. He has threatening to march off the job and was dragging his poor wife with him. He was claiming he under-quoted the job and was demanding 300% more for the job than what he quoted me.

Again ... the house has too big, ceilings too high and apparently, the house was just too dirty. I called him on his threat and asked him to leave. I got another professional cleaner for the next day.

So—*Oscar the Grouch* got no income, he wasted his time and mine, and he made sure I will never call that company again, for anything!

I have no idea why this man joined the services industry if he didn't want to service others. I have no idea how he was approved as a franchisee. This man will fail, no matter how many enquiries the franchisor sends to him, he will burn them.

The Gold

- These quoting systems are proven. They are fool proof.

- I know because I built them. They were the foundation that grow my business.

- It is foolish to think you can ignore the reality that you need a professional sales system to grow your business you will fail.

Chapter 11
The Quote

An effective quoting system will make or break your business. There is no other factor in the service industry that impacts your business more than the system you are using for giving quotes to customers.

This quoting system is a process of little things that make a big difference. It is not hard, by no means complicated, nor does it need any special sales skills. It is a system that can be followed by anyone, but you do have to stick to the system.

In this chapter, we will deal with the first three steps:

- Step #1—The Phone Call
- Step #2—The Appointment
- Step #3—The Personalised Quote

All too often, business owners don't even have a quoting system. They treat it like an intrusion into their day—stopping them from doing the *real work*. Whether that is washing dogs, cleaning cars, fixing computers, cleaning carpets, or just *running the business*.

It is an annoying chore that they have to do. Unfortunately, that is exactly how it feels to the customer when they inquire about getting a quote from them.

Bob And Carol

Let me share a story about Bob and Carol. Bob and Carol had a home cleaning business for over five years. Their business was booming. They had a great client base, excellent income, high hourly rate, and most importantly the work-family life balance they had always dreamed about. Their secret was quite simple, the foundations were our quoting systems.

All the little things that made a big difference.

When Bob and Carol got an enquiry they always followed the same systems. When the message was received, Bob immediately stopped what he was doing, found a quiet spot, got out his diary, sorted out his attitude, put a smile on his face, and returned the clients' call within 15 minutes.

During the call, Bob was always polite, friendly, and helpful. He NEVER quoted over the phone and always booked a face-to-face appointment with the client within 48 hours.

Most of the time we will do it the same day if the client is available.

If the client pressured him give an estimate over the phone, he would decline. It is impossible to *guess* how dirty or clean someone's house is without seeing it for yourself. History taught Bob that if he does quote over the phone, it will likely be WRONG and only creates a conflict with his client before he starts.

Nine out of ten clients are happy for him to do a face-to-face quote as it sends a powerful message—they *are* important. Book your face-to-face quote ASAP, but no later than 48 hours from the initial phone call.

Next, Bob and Carol turn up on time, in their *clean and tidy* uniforms (they kept clean spares in their car to use just for quoting). They have their signed vehicle or trailer and their business cards in hand as they knock on the door. They hand their new client their business card and introduce themselves.

They then ask the client, "Can you show us through your home and show us exactly what you want us to help you with?"

They then shut up and listen.

They take out their large quote book and write down everything that the clients tell them.

They always asked the client:

- *"Is this a one-off service or a regular service?"*

- *"Is there anything else you want done. Like on the top of the cupboards for example?"*

- *"Is there any one area that you personally would like us to focus on?"*

- *"Have you used another services provider? Is there anything you didn't like about their work?"*

- *"How often were you planning to use our services, weekly, fortnightly or monthly?"*

Once they have gone through the home with the customer, asked all the questions, and have a clear picture of exactly what their new client wants and expects, they put together a full, *written quote.* They will always present the client with two options that suit their needs.

They got the job on 92% of their quotes, which has been a solid conversion rate for them over many years.

When you use this quoting system it will positively impact your business like nothing else!

Why does this very simple system work so effectively?

- The home service provider is building a relationship with their client. The client gets to see the people who will be responsible to caring for their home.

- Trust is built on the professional appearance and attitude.

- By actively listening to their client they can provide a personalised quote that delivers exactly what is important to that person.

- There is NO STANDARD service; service expectations are a personal expectation of the individual client.

- The majority of service providers don't even meet their potential new clients when they quote.

- The client sees value for money, everything is in black and white.

- There are very few complaints. The client and the business owner are on the same page. Everyone has the same expectations.

- We found at James Home Services when there was a customer

complaint, nine out of ten times our franchisee had not supplied a written quote. Most complaints were usually a communication problem more than a service provider doing a poor job.

- The business owner is investing time with their client to demonstrate the quality of their services before they ask them to give them money.

The Gold

- All too often, business owners don't even have a quoting system.

- Their secret was quite simple, the foundations were our quoting systems. All the little things that made a big difference.

- The first three steps:

  - Step #1—The Phone Call
  - Step #2—The Appointment
  - Step #3—The Personalised Quote

- Smile and return the clients' call within 15 minutes.

- Turn up on time, in *clean and tidy* uniforms.

- NEVER quote over the phone, but always book a face-to-face appointment within 48 hours.

- Ask the client: *"Can you walk us through your home and show us exactly want you want us to help you with?"*

- There is NO STANDARD service, make it personal.

- Invest time with your client to demonstrate the quality of your services before you ask them to give you money, build a trustworthy relationship.

Chapter 12
Closing The Sale

Many small business owners don't understand the need to close a sale. They will spend a ton of time talking to the potential client, put together a comprehensive quote, and then not actually close the sale. It's a bit of smoke and mirrors.

Most service providers see themselves as the *Mowing Guy,* the *Pet Groomer,* or the *Car Detailer,* and definitely NOT as a salesperson. This is the first issue that needs to be dealt with. If you are in business, you had better get into sales or very quickly you will no longer be in business.

If you have no sales you have no business, no matter how good of a gardener you are. Regardless of what you may think, the clients are not going to be banging on your door begging to buy your *product.*

"It's Not My Fault"

I have coached hundreds of service business owners over 20 years and the most consistent area of concern for most of them is converting their quotes to actual business. It can be very disheartening to go do a quote and never hear form the client again.

The business owner creates a movie in their head about what may have happened with the quote. He imagines that he was underquoted, that the client was a tire-kicker, or that the customer did it for themselves. But these are only guesses. The only way to know for sure is to ask for the business. If you are going to ask, you may as well ask while you are still there. But there is a right and wrong way to ask for the job.

The Assumed Alternative Close

Historically, if a business owner was getting 90% of the quotes, they are likely following the quoting system 100%. They were expected NOT to convert all the quotes, not everybody is going to buy from you. They would certainly be using the *Assumed Alternative Close*:

"I can fit your dog in for a wash on Tuesday or Wednesday, which one suits you best?"

The *Assumed Alternate Close* asks the closing question with two keys. Firstly, it offers the buyer two options. Secondly, it assumes one of the options suits the buyer's needs.

It is backed by a positive attitude that assumes the client is ready to select one of the options offered by the service provider. The decision is made, and the appointment is booked in.

If a service business owner is converting 60% of their quotes, they are probably following the quoting process until they get to the close.

They are at least closing but it is most likely an open-ended close such as, *"When would you like your carpet cleaned?"*

When you do this, you are giving the customer a chance to think about it, and yourself an OUT from closing the sale.

All you achieve is raising all the problems. The client now has the chance to think about it, "When will I fit the cleaning into my busy week?"

If a business owner is converting only 30% of their quotes, they are at least turning up to do the quote but not closing at all. As a matter of fact, they are probably simply doing a verbal quote or leaving the written quote with the client and waiting for them to ring them back.

Roughly 30% will still ring back without a close. One question can create a 300% improvement in this business. It may seem hard to believe that an *Assumed Alternative Close* question can take a business from struggling to booming. But it does.

Now if the business is only getting 10% conversion from enquiry to converted quote, they are most likely quoting over the phone. The operator who does this is trying to avoid rejection or is unaware of the importance of the sales process. Either way, the business is doomed for failure.

You Are Going To Have To ASK For The Business

What is a *close*? Isn't that something those scary salespeople do? To put it very simply a close is asking for the business. If you want people to hire you, like it to or not, you are going have to ask for the sale.

Remember, the first half of your quoting process is actually about creating trust and building a quote that fits your clients' needs and/ or wants.

After you confirm that your quote is exactly what your client wants it is important that you offer them two options in your close—this is called an *alternative close*. It is either *Option A* or *Option B*.

Example #1

"Mrs Jackson, I can cover everything you would like done. Would you prefer our fortnightly service for $99 ... or our more popular weekly service for $89?"

Example #2

Mr Jones, I can fit your car in for a regular clean, would Thursday at 9 ... or Wednesday at 10 suit you better?

The *Assumed Alternative Close* makes the decision process easier for the client. It is about which of the two options suits best. It is not very complex, offer two options with a positive expectation. This works 90% of the time.

Often times, you will get the client booked in then and there. All you have to do is ask. When you ask for sale this way there are only two options: either your new client says,

"YES please."

or they say,

"No thank you."

What do you do if they say *No*? Firstly, they will most likely tell you *why*. But, if they don't tell you why, then you should ask,

"Is there a reason you are not going with our service?"

You might be surprised by the answer …

Then listen to their concerns and offer two additional options that address the issue such as:

Example #1

Mrs. Jackson says, *"I would like a weekly service, but I only have a budget of $80 per week for cleaning."*

You respond with two options:

"Mrs Jackson, I can help you with that, for your $80 budget, I can rotate the cleaning of the two bathrooms to every second week. Would you prefer an appointment on Monday at 9.30 … or on Tuesday at 2?"

Example #2

Mrs. Jackson says, "Neither of those days suits me."

You ask: *"Is there a particular day you had in mind?"*

Mr Jones: *"Yes, I wanted it done on a Friday. I like to have it clean for the weekend."*

Your response: *"I can help you, would you prefer 9.30am … or is 2.15pm more suitable?"*

Remember, your investment in a thorough quoting system is the vital foundation to closing the sale. When you invest time by asking questions, listening to your client, and answering their concerns, your solutions will be the best result for them.

It is easy to use the *Assumed Alternative Close* when you understand exactly what your clients wants because you have listened.

The Gold

- Many small business owners don't understand the need to close a sale.

- Most service provider see themselves as the *Mowing Guy,* the *Pet Groomer,* or the *Car Detailer* and definitely NOT as a salesperson. This is the first issue that needs to be dealt with.

- If you are in business, you better get into sales or very quickly you will not be in business anymore.

- Historically, if a business owner was getting 90% of his quotes, they were following the quoting system 100%.

- If you are going to ask for the business, you may as well ask while you are there.

- Whether you like it to or not, if you want people to give you money you have to ask for it.

- The stronger the trust and the better the fit your quote is the better strike rate on your quotes you will get.

- After you confirm that you quote is exactly what your client wants it is important that you offer them two options in your close. This is called an *Assumed Alternative Close—* either *Option A* or *Option B.*

Chapter 13
Delivering On Your Promises

The long-term success of your business will run directly parallel to the success of the relationships you build with your clients. Trust is the foundation to any successful relationship. In the home service industry trust is vital; your clients trust you with everything important to them. Whether it is their home, car, garden, or their dog. If you damage the trust, you will lose the client.

A professional service provider always does what they say they were going to do. You must do as you've promised, always. Trust is all about constantly delivering on your promises.

Once you've won the client, you have to get down to the business of delivering the promises.

Your Word

Your marketing has made promises both stated or unstated. You supplied your written quote that documented exactly what you are going to deliver to your client. It is time to deliver.

But, where do you start in guaranteeing that you deliver on your promises? It's the little things that make a big difference in how you are perceived by your clients.

Roughly 68% of clients who change their service provider do so because of the perceived indifference that they feel from their provider.

That being said, if your clients feel like you don't care about them then you should expect to have problems.

Your Image

Let's start with the non-stated promises. Your professional image is a promise. Be sure that a professional salesperson turns up every time—arrive on time, all staff (including you) should be in full uniform, and greet your client with a professional, positive attitude every single time.

This should happen every time you service every client and on every occasion. Do not get complacent once a client is booked in for a regular service.

Frequently, the business owner thinks that everything is perfect with the client, then drops their presentation standards. Your clients always notice your uniform, or lack thereof. If you look like you have dropped personal presentation your clients will start to look at your work with a more critical eye.

The Written Quote

The original written quote is a tool that enables you to deliver the promise both in the short-term and in the long-term. You can use the written quote as a checklist to guarantee that you and your staff are delivering the service that you originally promised.

In addition, when the first job is complete, ask your client to confirm that you have supplied everything that was quoted. If you did miss anything, then remedy the issue before you leave the job. Be absolutely sure they are satisfied before you leave.

The written quotes are protection for both the business owner and the client. If you do get a complaint, make your first reference to your written quote. Check to see if s the complaint is covered within your written quote.

If it is, then fix the problem immediately and be sure to apologize for the mistake. If you can even throw in a little extra work or a small discount on their next service, that would be great!

On the other hand, if the area of the complaint was not covered in your initial quote, show the quote to the client and explain exactly that was quoted for. Explain that this issue was not covered and offer to do the extra service for an extra charge or if the concern can be fixed quickly offer to do it free of charge.

Be very careful not to seem condescending or annoyed in this situation. We all make mistakes, it's how you handle them that leaves your mark on the client either positive or negative.

Attention To Detail

You have to be pragmatic in your evaluation of the standards of the services which you provide. Become your own biggest critic. Develop a keen eye for attention to detail.

Always look for the bit you may have missed before your client sees it. Be systematic in how you supply your practical services. Cleaning, pet grooming, lawn mowing or window washing always follow the same process, every time with every client.

Find a practical process that works best for you and stick with it every time you clean a house, wash a dog, polish a car, clean the carpets, or fix the computer. The more consistent you and your staff are with your practical procedures, the easier it is to maintain the highest level of service.

It also makes it easier if all staff can move between clients' homes because they understand exactly how your practical business systems operate, and what your expectations of them are. You may even consider making an actual checklist that is to be followed with each and every service.

Gold Medal Service:
The Expectation *Not* The Exception

Once you have delivered on the promise, then go the extra mile; take your services to another level. At *James Home Services* we called it *Gold Medal Service*. Go a little bit further, give a little bit more. Do something special that will really *WOW* your clients.

This can be as simple as bringing the washing in off the line before the rain starts, bringing a treat for their dog, or a personalized card over the holidays or on their birthday. Maybe a random *thank you for being our client* note and a box of chocolates.

It Really Is The Little Things

Alan and Trish were a couple who had a very successful home cleaning business within James' Home Services network for over 10 years. They had both left corporate banking careers behind them to work together in their business. Their client base was excellent. Most of their clients had been with them since the first year, and they had never lost a client for any reason.

In fact, their clients happily paid them top dollar because they had a proven track record of always delivering on their promises.

The trust between them and their customers was 100%. Why? Because for over 10 years they delivered the promise every single time, for every single client. They walked the walk and talked the talk.

Without fail, they consistently did all the little things that made the big difference to their customers. They followed the proven systems to the letter; in fact, they never even thought about not following those systems.

There was one special little extra that they added to their systems.

Alan and Trish were truly humble.

They honestly appreciated the success they were having in their business because of how much it changed their life for the better. And, they knew that their success, as well as their happiness, was a result of the strong relationships with their valuable clients.

They had no success without the clients and they knew it. With this in mind, they showed their appreciation to their clients every week with a simple gift. Oftentimes, the gift would be flowers from their own garden, presented beautifully on the kitchen bench. On other occasions, it was simply a minty, a lolly, or a chocolate left with a personal note.

On birthdays, Easter or Christmas there was always a card. Taking the time to think about their customers and doing that little extra to show they valued them gave huge dividends over their years of running a very successful business.

The bottom line is that there is only one person's opinion that matters. That is that of the clients who are paying you. If they are happy, then you will also end up as happy business owner.

How do you really know if your clients are happy? There is only one way. You have to ask them and keep on asking them. It may sound corny, but these are very important questions to ask:

"Mrs. Jones are you 100% happy with the services we are providing? Is there any area of the service you would like us to improve?"

Ask them face-to-face, then ask again in emails and text messages. I strongly recommend you even employ someone external to ask the clients on your behalf. This feedback will give you positive reinforcement on the things you are doing really well, but it will also give you clear directions on what areas of your business could use improvement.

Furthermore, it is then vial that you listen to this feedback and act on it.

If you have staff members let them know when they get great feedback and make them aware of the areas of needed improvement.

Make sure your clients know you are listening to the good and the bad—it keeps the lines of communication open, so they keep sharing with you.

Ask, ask, ask, ask, ask, and ask again. Then listen and take action.

The Gold

- The long-term success of your business will be directly connected to the success of relationships you build with your clients.

- Trust is the foundation to any successful relationship.

- A professional service provider does what they say they are going to do.

- If your client feels you don't care, then you should expect to have problems.

- Your professional image is a promise.

- You clients always notice your uniform, or lack thereof.

- The original written quote is a tool that empowers you to deliver the promise both in the short-term and in the long-term.

- The written quotes are protection for both the business owner and the client.

- You must be pragmatic in your evaluation of the standards of the services you provide—become your own biggest critic.

- Do something special that personally *WOWs* your clients.

- The bottom line is that there is only one person's opinion that matters—the client's.

- Ask, ask, ask, ask, ask, and ask again. Then listen and take action.

Chapter 14
Document Your Procedures

Everyone has a process and procedure for everything they do. We all do. Our alarm clocks wake us up, some of us get right in the shower while others stumble to the coffeepot. Or, maybe you hit the snooze button a few times?

Surely, you have a procedure that gets everyone in the house up, dressed, and out the door every morning. This process is how you make sure no one forgets anything, and everyone is where they need to be when they need to be there, right?

What happens if you are sick and can't get out of bed? What happens to the morning routine in your house?

Be honest ...

Your business is no different. Everything you do must be documented. From start to finish—what is your procedure for doing the absolute best job you can? Think about it.

The amazing thing is that most business owners don't document their procedures at all. Perhaps they don't even recognise the need to do so *because it's all my head*. The key problem with that concept is that nothing can be delegated to anyone because no one knows exactly how you do what you do. The business will always be handicapped in its future growth.

It's Amazing When You Think About It

I have been in franchising for a very long time and have been approached by hundreds of *Wannabe Franchisors*. Most of them had a business that was making good money and they all had grand plans for expansion. Less than 5% of them made the effort to document their procedures.

Without documentation, you have no system, just an idea that is still floating around in your head and the heads of your key staff members.

When I'm coaching these potential franchisors, one of my first group of questions is:

"How do you answer your business phones?"

"How do you teach new people this skill?"

"Can you show me the manual for this?"

You may think it is simple to answer the phone. You may even believe this is being unduly patronising. The reality is that many small business owners and their employees don't handle their phone enquiries effectively. So, an effective system is the first necessity of any service business. If you have a documented system, then you can accurately measure the results and improve your procedures as needed.

Your phone answering procedure should be a very straightforward. It is an easy first step in the documentation of your business systems and procedures.

You may be surprised by the number of variations there are when it comes to answering the phone when you document what is going on. Training on your phone system should be just as straightforward. This is why it should be your starting point. The systems and the training of those systems need to be documented.

You may have no plans to expand to a national network. You may be happy to keep your business local. That is fine, but there will be days when you want to have the day off or when your business starts to boom that you want to employ others to service more clients.

The only way to deliver consistency across the board is with written manuals.

A Huge Undertaking?

Documenting manuals can be quite daunting for many business owners. The thought of it can be enough to discourage many from even attempting it.

In the beginning, you can use a very simple system to document your procedures. Later, these can evolve to professional manuals if needed. Manuals will evolve and develop.

There are processes already in place that you may be unaware of until you start documenting everything.

Video Manuals

Video is a very effective place to start, especially for your practical service skills. It is an excellent way to document and to demonstrate what you do and exactly how you do it. These can be used to train new employees, as a reminder for yourself, etc.

Video all of your practical procedures.

It can be how you wash a car, clip a dog, mow a lawn, or even clean a bathroom. You will be amazed at how much you do on autopilot and how these videos will catch every single detail.

Your videos don't have to be professional, but I recommend you attempt to record each practical procedure at least twice. Then take your time in evaluating exactly how you are doing your services.

There may be differences between your two recordings or you may observe something that can be improved. Test, measure, and then improve as needed.

Checklists

Checklists do work as well. They are direct and constant reminders of what needs to be done. Simple checklists can be the foundations of a more detailed manual as they evolve.

A checklist on each service gives clarity for your staff members. The procedures of the start and finishing ritual is a vital process to being prepared for the daily routine.

Number each process from # 1 to the very end. Include every detail; even the assumed details such as the friendly greeting for the customer, bringing all necessary equipment, or carefully placing the dog on the grooming table.

Even the quoting system can be lead from a checklist. Your checklist should follow from first contact to booking the final appointment.

One of the most effective uses of a checklist we had in our business was the *9 Simple Steps to An Extraordinary Service Business.* We had the checklist everywhere.

And I mean everywhere!

We placed stickers on the insides of the vans and trailers so that each time the franchisee opened his or her van or trailer they would see the *9 Simple Steps to An Extraordinary Service Business*. It was a constant reminder of the expectations of running a business with the *James'* name attached to it.

There was no way you could not be reminded of those steps on which the foundations of our business were built. The conscious and subconscious reminders were at eye-level, literally, all day every day.

It was impossible to *not* be reminded of these steps.

We had large stickers on the inside doors of our trailers and vans. The steps were on smaller business card size stickers that we placed on the quote book, back of the mobile phone and on the driver's sun visor. We even had palm cards that fitted into the franchisee's wallet.

Structured Manuals

Professionally compiled manuals will become a huge asset to your business. You may not really understand in the early days how important they can be to the success of your business. I understand that if you are starting as a one-man band business, it may seem like a waste of your time to put these manuals together.

However, the manuals will become the tool that can give you long-term success in your business. They are vital to servicing a large client base. They will empower you to delegate roles within your business and release yourself from the day-to-day hands-on work. What's the point of owning and operating your own business if you can't take a day off once in a while?

The Gold

- Everything you do in your business must be documented.

- Without documentation, you have no system. Just an idea that is floating around in your head and the heads of your key staff members.

- The procedures and the training of those systems must be documented.

- Documenting manuals can be quite daunting for many business owners.

- Professionally complied manuals will become a huge asset to your business.

Chapter 15
Organising Your Business

I know organising your business sounds like a really uninteresting topic. It may even sound like a lot of wasted time that you really can't spare—sitting around doing nothing when you could be doing something useful like mowing lawns, cleaning cars or houses, delivering coffee, fixing computers, cleaning windows or grooming dogs. Making money, right?

I also can understand that you could be actually delivering services that have a direct cash return for your energy and certainly, a clear return on the investment of your time. This is why most business owners choose to place *organising their business* at the bottom of their daily to do list.

That was exactly how I operated in the early days of my service business. The first year I was running my mobile car cleaning business was completely unorganised. I would get paid mostly in cash and simply pay for the things I needed as I went. I did document all my income at the end of each day and kept the receipts for expenses that I threw in a shoe box.

At the end of that first year of business, I went to my accountant and handed him the box. He wasn't very impressed with my method of tracking my business expenses.

He gave me a very long-winded lecture about why it is so vital to keep professional business records. At the time I was uninterested, but deep down, I knew he was right. I certainly wasn't running an effective business. I had to accept that the only way to make the most of my business was to get my business organised.

And I mean really, really organised.

Organisation is not just about the paperwork; It is about the preparation; It is about the structure you absolutely must create in all aspects of your business.

In the service industry, your most valuable asset is time. Essentially, it's what you are selling.

Don't get me wrong, I understand that technically you are selling your services, but you are also giving your clients their TIME back. That is priceless to most of them! If your business is unorganised you are wasting the product you are selling, which makes absolutely no sense.

Time management is a vital skill in developing an effective service business. It's actually very simple—the more effectively you are able to manage your time, the *more real work* you can get done. Which means you can make more money.

A diary is a necessity. It can be either paper or digital. A daily and work worksheet are also a huge help to see where you can fit your work into your week.

Nesting Your Appointments

The first place to start is with *nesting* your appointments. What do I mean by *nesting*? Book each day's clients as close in proximity to one another as possible. Instead of driving from one town to the next and then back again, swap the appointments around to put them in a more practical order. You can greatly reduce your travel time by doing this.

You may even be able to reduce your travel enough to add an extra client or two each day or get home an hour early each day if you prefer? This is one of the fastest and easiest ways to improve your time management by at least 20%.

When you book new client appointments, offer them spots that are the most geographically desirable for your business. If you currently have regular clients that are out of the way or creating unnecessary driving, ask them to move to a more workable appointment time. It may be time to let some clients go if they are uncooperative.

Sometimes, you have to look rationally at the amount of time a client is COSTING you if you are driving a long way to get to them. If you are travelling too much you will be working for nothing, the profit in your business will be going into costs instead of profits. The more you travel the higher your costs.

Quoted Hourly Rate

The hourly rate you are currently quoting to your clients is the second most vital ingredient to designing a successful service business. Quote too low, and you will not survive long-term. Quote too high, and you will not survive long-term.

It is not about being the cheapest nor dearest. It is pitching your quote at the upper middle for your industry standards.

The real secret is to deliver a high-quality service and charge for it accordingly.

Top quality service is always in high demand. Be pragmatic in your commercial decisions around building your regular client base. Your regular client base will make or break your business. A well organised, profitable client base creates an effective, profitable business.

Make Proper Use Of Your Time

It is very important that you make proper use of your time during your work day. Don't waste time chatting too much to clients or your employees. If you have employees, keep them on the time table. Make sure they are clear how much time is booked for each job.

A simple checklist to make sure everyone is clear on exactly what is expected of them on each job will make your expectations very clear. There will be no misunderstandings about what they are supposed to do.

Client Base

As you build your client base, document that client base. Your client records are easily one of the most highly valuable assets of your business. No client base, no business asset. It is one thing to say that your clients are long-term, but nothing proves the point more than three years of records for every service you have ever provided to them.

You can use electronic records or old school paper client cards. The most important issue is that you maintain them and update them every day with thorough details.

But What Should You Record?

- **Client Contact Details** such as name, address, phone numbers, email, *Facebook*, etc.

- **Service Details** such as appointment time, frequency of service, and any other details that may help you keep track of the details (i.e. where the keys are kept, size of the house, how payment is made, children and pets names, hobbies, as well as birthdays). One day you will hope to sell your business and these records will add to the value of your business.

Paperwork

Keeping your paperwork up to date is also a necessity.

There are many, very good small business bookkeeping systems in the market place. Whether you prefer electronic or hard copy data, choose a system that works best for you.

Then update your books each afternoon or evening. It will only take about 15 minutes if you do it daily. I recommend you get some direction from your own accountant to handle your tax responsibilities.

Cash Flow

Believe it or not, cash flow is much more important than overall profit. There is no point in supplying a service if you don't get paid for it. Organise your payment when you book an appointment in. It doesn't really matter how you are paid, as long as you get paid for the services you are providing.

The worst area to get into problems is if there is confusion on how much the job is going to cost the client, which is why EVERY SINGLE job should have a written quote. The other is if the client doesn't't have a clear understanding of when and how you expect them to pay you. Be very clear in your communication on this.

No business owner wants to be chasing outstanding money. It is the probably the absolute most frustrating waste of time there is. If someone doesn't pay on time, don't keep servicing them.

If you have only 20% of your clients that are always behind, you will quickly find that you always have one month's turnover outstanding. This will translate into the majority of your profit NOT being in your bank account. Never a good position to be in ...

I have seen many business owners get themselves into huge financial problems all because they won't ask for the money. It's very important that you get comfortable asking for the payment. Your client had no issues asking you to perform the work for them, they really shouldn't have a problem paying for that work either:

"Mr Smith, I accept payment by cash, card ... or bank transfer when I complete the job. Which would you prefer?"

The Gold

- Organising your business may sound like a lot of wasted time when you could be doing something more useful like mowing lawns, cleaning cars or houses, delivering coffee, fixing computers, cleaning windows, or grooming dogs.
  But it isn't, it will make you more money.

- I had to accept that the only way to make the most of my business was to get my business organised.

- Organisation is not just about the paperwork. It is about preparation and structure in all areas of your business.

- Time management is a vital skill in developing an effective service business. If you save time you have more time to sell to clients.

- When you book new clients in only offer the spots that are the most effective for your business.

- Throughout your working day, be sure to make proper use of your time.

- There are many good small business bookkeeping systems on the market. Whether you prefer electronic or hard copy, choose the one that best suits you and your business.

- Cash flow is more important than profit. There is no point in supplying a service if you don't get paid for it.
  Organise your payment when you book an appointment in.

- No one wants to be chasing outstanding money, it is the biggest waste of time possible. If someone doesn't pay on time, don't keep servicing them.

- You cannot be afraid to ask for the payment.

Chapter 16
Follow-Up With Your Clients

Your returning client base is the foundation of your business and their value cannot be understated. As such, the level of service you deliver to these clients will decide whether your business is a success or not. The only people who can give you true feedback on your performance as a company are these clients, not the clients that didn't use your services, or only used them once.

No News Is Not Good News

Following up with your clients is a key ingredient of the ongoing growth of your business and absolutely must be part of your system. The follow-up is all about taking the responsibility to initiate the contact with your clients.

When you take that responsibility, it becomes a very powerful tool to develop and maintain the key relationships in your business.

If you are proactively getting valuable feedback, listening to your clients, and then acting based on their comments to improve your level of service, you are guaranteed to be exceeding your customers' expectations.

The power comes from putting yourself out there to get the upfront feedback; be it good or bad. The level of respect your clients will give you in return is amazing. This simple action will take you to the elite level of service providers.

It does seem very simple, doesn't it?

"How did everything go today/yesterday?"

"How can we improve our service for you?"

"What areas can we do better?"

"What areas did we do well in?"

Why Don't Many Service Business Owners Do This?

They are afraid of what they may find out.

The fear of hearing the negative, or the possibility that the client may say they don't want to use their services again is far more frightening than the payoff of the positive feedback.

They may even feel that they are being pushy and will upset the clients. The fear of possible rejection can be very disabling force.

Debbie

The fear of rejection can be so disabling in fact, that I have seen many people like Debbie, a pet groomer, who would *never* proactively ask a client to book a service or make a call to see if owners needed anything. Debbie was an excellent dog groomer; she absolutely loved what she did.

She loved the dogs and their owners—her clients—but her business was failing. Her client base just wasn't growing. She had plenty of new client enquiries, but she wasn't converting these into regular clients because she was afraid to ask for the future appointment.

As the franchisor, we had a system in place to support our Franchisees, part of those systems was contacting our clients and getting feedback on our franchisees.

We had a system of questions that we asked the clients about the service they were receiving

There were 20 targeted questions that verified that the franchisee was following our systems and delivering the level of service that we expected for our clients. The follow-up systems were designed to help us help our franchisees succeed. The clients very quickly gave honest feedback on the performance of our business owners.

When we did the follow-up training with Debbie, her clients certainly told us what was happening with her business. They consistently rated the quality of her work as a 10 out of 10. They said she had a great attitude—again 10 out of 10. They said that she presented and communicated very professionally—9 out of 10.

However, when we asked them whether or not they used her services regularly, our results were not nearly as good—*only 2 out of 10*.

As you can imagine, with such excellent feedback on the other factors, such a low rating on regular service was shocking. Of course, we asked why they didn't use her service again and nearly every single one of them said just about the same thing:

"I would ... but I haven't seen her since she washed my dog!"

The next question we asked: *"Did Debbie ask you if you would like a weekly or fortnightly service?"*

Consistently, the answer was, *"No, but if she isn't too busy, I would love to do that!"*

Debbie got eight return clients from the ten people we rang for follow-up. I did ask her why she didn't follow the system and directly book them in?

Her answer was surprising:

"I can't handle the rejection. When someone says no to me it is like an arrow through my heart. They have to ask me to book them in for me to do that."

Only two out of every ten clients were actively asking the question. The other eight were waiting or expecting Debbie to take responsibility to book them or follow-up with them about booking their next appointment. She was literally losing 80% of her regular clients by leaving out a simple question.

Just because she was afraid they might say *No* to her.

Once she got over her fear of rejection and began following up with her clients on a regular basis, Debbie saw a huge improvement in her business! Her client base and zone grew rapidly because she figured out what the problem was and acted to fix the situation.

She began following up with all her clients, and she was getting more repeat business than she ever thought possible. Without making this change, Debbie would not have lasted another three months in business.

Why Should You Follow-Up With Your Clients?

Firstly, it can be very reassuring. If you are doing a good job, your clients will be more than happy to hear from you. You will get to hear all about the great work you have done. Roughly 95% of your feedback will be positive; while the other 5% will be the areas that need to be improved. That is very good by any standards. If you got 95% on a test at school your mum would have been very happy.

If you have followed the first five steps of these nine steps, you should have no problems doing the follow-up. But if you or your staff members missed anything, then you can be on the front foot to fix the problems before the client has to complain to get the problem fixed or worst, they will leave permanently.

Doing regular follow-up with your clients will ensure that you have up to date information to meet your client's needs. Their situations or wants may change; their finances may change. Perhaps, they can now afford a more comprehensive service, or to have it done more often. There may be a new addition, or mum may just need more help around the house or garden. In any case the follow-up is simply elite customer service.

Your clients are busy people, that is why they use a professional home service business.

Take the responsibility to follow-up with your clients, it will turbo charge your business to a truly professional level.

The Gold

- Your returning client base is the foundation of your business.

- When you take responsibility for the follow-up, it becomes a very powerful tool to develop and maintain the key relationships in your business.

- If you are proactively getting valuable feedback, listening to your clients, and then taking action to improve your level of service, you are guaranteed to be exceeding your customers' expectations.

- The clients will very quickly give honest feedback on your performance.

- If you have previously done a good job the clients will be more than happy to hear from you.

- Your regular follow-up will ensure you have up-to-date information to meet your client's needs. Their situations or wants may have changed.

- Take responsibility to follow-up with your clients regularly.

Chapter 17
Continue To Deliver

Continuing to deliver on your promises can be even more challenging over your long-term relationship with the client. The more frequently you perform the same service for the same client, the more likely you are to fall short. Like all relationships you have to keep investing time and energy into it. There is no room for complacency with your clients—the biggest danger to your client base is *perceived indifference*.

What is *perceived indifference*? It is very simple, it is when your clients feel like you are indifferent to them, to their need or wants. Basically, they *feel* that you don't care about them.

You may say, *"No, that's not me! I love all my clients and they love me!"* Although that may be true, it is not about what you think but more about their perceptions about the relationship.

Very simply, you must maintain your standards, or they will interpret any drops in quality as a sign that you are taking them for granted. Little things really do make a big difference. Your clients notice the little things that you do for them and they will notice the little things you stop doing as well.

Folding The Toilet Paper

A great example of the little things making a big difference can be found in the folding of the toilet paper. Toilet paper folding can't really be that important, can it? I think it can.

In our home cleaning system, our franchisees would fold the toilet paper into a nice tidy little triangle. You may have seen it in quality hotels.

Our testing showed that this was one, very simple way to show the client that we were a little bit more upmarket than our competitors. Of course, they had to do everything else perfectly, but the toilet paper fold was the little thing that you might call the icing on the cake. It was that little thing that showed our attention to detail—that we took the time to fold the toilet paper roll.

Graham And Beverly

Graham and Beverly were one of our long-term home cleaning franchisees who had been in business for over five years.

The whole business was reliant upon their long-term client base. Out of their many regular, weekly customers, they had never had a single compliant. They were excellent service providers.

As sometimes happens, they had an unexpected change in their personal situation. Beverly began having health issues and needed time away from the business to get well. They decided to cover the client base and hired an employee to cover her work load while she was off.

They decided they wanted to keep her health concerns private and chose not to tell their clients.

Graham was able to train the new staff member on the systems. She had a great attitude, had experience in cleaning, possessed a good eye for detail, and took the system training on board. She was perfect for the role, so much so that they even took on a few extra clients to cover her wages. It seemed like a great situation all around.

However, about three weeks into the new employee joining the team something strange happened! The clients started complaining. People who had been with them for years seemed to get very picky. It seemed as if they were going out of their way to find a lot of very small mistakes.

All the complaints were different—it wasn't just one thing that wasn't being done correctly that they were complaining about. Literally, each complaint was different. Graham had been personally overseeing the new employee's work and he honestly didn't think she was doing anything wrong. But they had five complaints called into the office in a week. All very minor issues, but complaints none-the-less.

What was really going on?

Our head office support made calls to the clients to ask them what the problem was.

Firstly, the new woman was not Beverly. Apparently, they felt she had abandoned them and they just loved her.

Believe it or not, the one thing they all mentioned was the toilet paper. *"Beverly always used to fold the toilet paper."*

From the customers perspective, the folding of the toilet paper was a little personal signature of Bev's. They didn't know that every franchisee in our system of 400 plus business owners were taught to fold the toilet paper. This step was part of our systems, but it stopped happening when Bev needed time out to convalesce.

I sat down with Graham and asked him if he was aware of the *folding the toilet paper* situation. He told me that he did train his new staff member on all the system standards but that he did notice she stopped doing it in the second week of her employment. She was working hard and was doing everything else at a high standard and he just didn't think it was a big enough deal to worry about it, so he let it go.

No one actually complained about the lack of a fold in their toilet paper, but they would find other, more serious issues to complain about. Things like missing in the area in front of the toilet or not moving the lounge when vacuuming. To the client, the non-folding of the toilet paper was a sign of a lack of attention to detail—that Graham and Bev were indifferent to the relationship.

So, how did we fix the drama of the folding of the toilet paper? The paper got folded. And then, the situation with Bev was explained to the customers. They really understood when we told them what was going on with Bev.

In fact, the head office was inundated with cards, gifts, and even flowers to forward to her. The great news is that Bev made a full recovery and all of her clients waited patiently for her return.

It is vital that you proactively communicate with your clients just how much you value them. Make a concerted effort to show them on a regular basis just how important they are to your business.

Remember, little things can make a big difference. Flowers, cards, gifts of the fragrance you use when you clean or remove spots, chocolates, or bringing the clothes in off the line are examples of those little things. Keep taking notice of the little things because your clients are definitely noticing.

Research shows 68% of your clients will leave because of *perceived indifference.*

Systematically deliver high quality service. If you drop your standards, you will lose your clients. And always, always invest the time to confirm you are delivering on your service promise.

The Gold

- Continuing to deliver on your promises can be even more challenging over the long-term.

- The biggest danger to your client base is perceived indifference.

- Perceived indifference is when your clients think that you don't care about their need or wants.

- Simply put, you must maintain the standards they are accustomed to or they will interpret any drops in quality as a sign that you are taking them for granted.

- To the client the non-folding of the toilet paper was a sign that Graham and Beverly were *indifferent* to the relationship.

- It is vital that you proactively communicate with your clients just how much you do value them.

- Consistently deliver high quality service. If you drop your standards, you will lose your clients.

Chapter 18
Ask Your Clients For The Referral

The greatest fans you will ever have in your business are your happy, loyal, and satisfied clients. These happy clients have an emotional connection not only to your business, but to you as well. They can be the best sales representatives you can possibly dream of.

If you are delivering on your promises and exceeding your customers' expectations, they will be more than happy to praise your services to their friends, family, and colleagues. Referrals from your current client base are easily one of the best ways to increase your business turnover, but most business owners are uncomfortable asking for referrals and in most cases, won't.

Most people don't mind being asked for the referral so long as they are happy with the service you provide.

Great service will get great referrals in return. They will happily recommend your business to other people they know.

Asking for the referral is as simple as asking this question:

"Do you have any friends or relatives who could benefit from our services?"

Or, perhaps something like this:

"Do you know anyone on your street/at your work who needs …? If we can organise the appointment on the same day around the same time, I could offer both of you a discount for saving me the time on travelling. Would you be kind enough to ask them on my behalf?

Or, maybe more like this if you are more comfortable with it:

"If you know anyone that I can help, would you mind giving them my number, or I'm happy to contact them directly if that would be easier for you?"

Word Of Mouth

Everyone always says that *word of mouth* travels fast. This is especially true in the service business. If you actively encourage your clients to sing your praises, then your business will prosper at a speed you cannot generate in any other way. Actively engaging your clients to help promote your business gives you a huge positive leverage; think of it as working smarter instead of harder.

Many service businesses will tell you that *word of mouth* is where most of their new clients come from.

The same businesses will tell you they don't have to ask for referrals. If you are getting referrals without asking for them, that is great, but you are likely only getting about 10% of the available possible referrals.

Many of your clients will assume you are too busy to take on new clients. When you actively ask for the referral it demonstrates to them that you are motivated to grow your business and will take excellent care of the person they refer to you. It brings up that trust thing we talked about earlier—if you do a good enough job for them, they will trust to take good care of their friends.

A Vested Interest

Your clients will become stakeholders in your business. They become fans, like being a fan of their favourite football team or television show. You become their car cleaner, their house cleaner, their pet groomer, their IT guy and they will cheer your success as your business grows.

Remember to always reward the clients who help you grow by

giving you the referrals. Give them small gifts such as flowers, cards, extra services, and most importantly, a big *thank you.*

Asking for referrals changed my business when I was a one-man band car-cleaning business.

I vividly recall implementing the plan. I gave myself the mission to ask every single client for a referral. It had a truly amazing response - I found that many of them would give me a name or referral upfront. Then on the following visits they would supply even more!

I found out that I had about four *true believers* who were clearly strong influencers within their circle of friends. Without fail, when they referred me to a friend or relative, that person always became a regular client.

It Only Takes One ...

I had a very well-known local property developer and real estate agent. His family had been in business in the region for over 75 years. They were heavily involved in the growth and development of the region during that period of time.

They had 75 years of credibility that gave them a huge ability to influence others. This business man became one of my biggest fans and my client base expanded rapidly as a result of his referrals and friends.

On top of that, my business became associated with his credibility and experienced a turbo charge from the support of this one businessman. That one person changed the course of my business for the better—it's amazing what one influential client can do!

When your business is in the early days many potential clients may have doubts about the likelihood that your business will be around in the future. In fact, they will frequently wait to see if you *make it.*

Once you get the referral support from key members of your community it takes your business credibility to the next level. All because I got up the courage to implement the *ask for the referral* as a system in my business.

Social media has taken the *ask for the referral* concept to the next level.

Encourage your clients to refer your services on their social media pages. Encourage them to comment on your *Facebook* page, or your other social media pages. Ask their permission to post before and after photos of the services you do provide for them. Ask your clients to share the posts with their *Facebook* friends as well.

It is up to you to become proactive about asking for referrals from your clients. They are not going to throw new business your way without you asking for it. If you get out of your comfort zone and take action to implement this procedure your business will very quickly grow to the next level.

The Gold

- The greatest fans you will ever have in your business are your happy, loyal, satisfied clients.

- Referrals from your client base are one of the best ways to increase your business turnover, but most people are uncomfortable when asking for one and in most cases, won't.

- Many of your clients assume you are too busy to take on new clients.

- Actively engaging your clients to help promote your business gives you a huge positive leverage. You will be working smarter rather than harder.

- Your clients will become stakeholders in your business. They become fans, like being a fan of their favourite football team or television show.

- Once you get the referral support from key members of your community, it takes your own business credibility to the next level.

- Social media can take the *ask for the referral* concept to the next level. Encourage your clients to refer your services on their own social media pages.

- It is up to you to become proactive about asking your current clients for referrals—no one is going to do this for you!

Chapter 19
Repeat The Process

Discipline is the fuel that will fire the long-term success of your business. It takes true discipline to stay focused on the long-term goals you have set for yourself and for your business. It is very easy for some people to get bored doing the same thing day in and day out. But I can tell you, your clients will never get bored with great service.

Your ability and willingness to repeat the process over and over again, with every single client, is the sign of a true professional. It takes true commitment to repeat this process. Sticking to your systems and building true foundations with a long-term commitment will give you an extraordinary home service business.

Change Is Not Always Good

Over the years, I have discovered that oftentimes people will change successful behaviours because they get bored. Bored with doing the same thing over and over again. They may even argue that they are *too creative* to be systematically repeating behaviours, no matter how successful those behaviours may be.

The question you must ask yourself is, *"Is the behaviour working for me?"* Are you getting the results you want from it? If yes—then KEEP DOING IT. If no—then change it.

Don't get me wrong, it is okay to change and adjust things as you go. However, never change a successful behaviour simply because you are bored with it. If you find yourself getting bored, then go back and redesign your business to take it to the next level or re-evaluate your family and business goals.

The day-to-day commitment it takes to consistently deliver a high-standard of service to your clients is about you directly connecting the goals you have set for your business with the goals you set for your family. There is a reason it is called a *family business.* The two are highly connected. When you understand this connection, you will find it easier to turn up each day and deliver the promise to your clients. It won't be a chore anymore but a passion that will make you proud.

Why do you to repeat all the steps?

Your business is a growing entity. It can never stay exactly the same. Things are always changing, but if you are systematically evolving your business you will grow with your business. There are key areas to keep a close eye on in each of the steps.

The 9 Secrets to Extraordinary
Service Business Success

#1- Design your Brand
#2-Market your Business every day
#3-Get the First Job
#4-Always deliver on your Promises
#5-Organise your Business
#6-Follow-up with your Clients
#7-Continue to Deliver
#8-Ask for the Referral
#9-Repeat the Process

#1—Design Your Brand

You can certainly build your own professional brand, but you must also maintain that brand.

Many small business owners get complacent with their image. They let their uniforms get worn and faded, run out of business cards and/or brochures, and don't bother investing in new ones.

As your business grows take the time to step back and take a look at how your clients *see* your business. The signage on your vehicles can fade and look tired. You may not notice, but your customers will definitely notice.

You may even see a need to update the look of your brand depending on how far your business has evolved since you started. You may even have a better idea of your target market and what will attract them.

#2—Market Your Business Every Day

The how-to market is now more easily available to the average family, home-based business.

The biggest challenge over time is that as many businesses grow, the owners stop investing each day in those *future* clients because they feel they don't need them anymore.

While it is true that you don't necessarily need the same level of business growth as you did in the initial start-up days, it is important to market back to clients who are using your services or have used your services in the past. It is about consolidating your businesses client base.

You do not want people to forget about you because the next business will be happy to fill in and take the business from you.

Social media is a vital area to invest in every day as well. If you get lazy and neglect your social media presence it will quickly open the door for others in your industry to get a foot hold in your market. It is vital to keep your social media presence current and updated with daily, useful information.

#3—Get The First Job

The ONLY way to get a regular client and build a client base is to "Get the First Job form the initial enquiry."

However, new clients should be given the same opportunities to use your business as your established clients. The same professional sales systems should be implemented with every client.

It is just as important to demonstrate your enthusiasm for new business. If you focus on getting the new client into your business and making them your future fans, your business will definitely grow.

#4—Always Deliver On Your Promises

Turning up and delivering on your promises goes a long way towards being successful.

Great business systems become effective habits. If you build a culture around systems that always deliver your promises to your clients, you are guaranteed success.

#5—Organise Your Business

Many of the organisation areas and administration skills may be better off outsourced; doing so also requires some careful organisation.

It is vital to keep your ducks in a row. Keeping outstanding accounts up to date is very important as well. No one can afford to supply services and chase the money. It is a waste of your time, energy, and even more money.

Systematically keep the accounts up to date.

#6—Follow-Up With Your Clients

The follow-up contact will also give you the opportunity to offer regular or additional services they are not currently taking advantage of.

Be proactive! Following up with your clients on a regular basis is very important. Your clients' feedback is the opportunity to maintain and grow these valuable relationships.

#7—Continue To Deliver

Remember, 68% of lost business is a result of the client feeling a perceived indifference from you.

Every business that stops showing the love to their clients, faces the risk that they will lose their business.

No clients, no business—it's very, very simple. Large, medium, or small businesses that get complacent in delivering will eventually fail.

#8—Ask For The Referral

You do have to ask for the referral.

You must get out of your comfort zone and ask the question. These are simple questions that can keep your business growing at a turbo charged rate.

#9—Repeat The Process

Sticking to your systems and building solid foundations with a long-term commitment will give you an extraordinary home service business.

Now, go back to step # 1 and do it all again.

The Gold

- Discipline is the fuel that will fire the long-term success of your business. It takes true discipline to stay focused on the long-term goals that you want to achieve with your business.

- I have found that people frequently change successful behaviours because they become bored with them.

- If you find yourself getting bored, then go back and redesign your business to take it to the next level or re-evaluate your family and business goals.

- The day-to-day commitment it takes to consistently deliver high-performance service to your clients is about you connecting the service you provide to your clients to the goals you set for your family and business.

- Your business is a growing entity. It can never stay exactly the same.

Chapter 20
To Grow Or Not To Grow?

That really is the question, isn't it?

Your business is booming. You have followed the *9 Steps*, and they worked. You made the investment and documented all your systems. You've even hit your sales targets and the goals you set for yourself and for your family. Life seems to be good, but you want to achieve more.

Now What?

Do you take the next leap of faith? Do you launch your business to the next level? Expand your territory? Evolve into another service your clients have been asking about?

What's next for you? Is it worth taking more risk?

Many successful business owners reach this milestone and can get a bit lost. This is the perfect time to refocus on your long-term goals. Stop and take the time to make a definite decision on where you want your business journey to end.

Growth for the sake of growth is a pointless path that will lead you nowhere you want to be.

Decide where you want your business to take you, then take consistent, focused action in that direction.

There is a danger that your successful business could end up being the wheel that you are *chained to*. If you are not careful, you will look up one day and realize you have been transformed into a *slave* to the business that you brought to life.

In my previous book, *Balance: How to Make Your Business and Family Life Work Together, I* deal with the challenge of making your business work for your family.

I strongly recommend all business owners take the time to get clarity on what long term outcomes you want for your family life from your business.

Stuck In Survival Mode?

Many business owners can get caught up in the *survival mode* that drove them in the early days. There is a fear motivation that oftentimes *helped* them survive in the beginning. It is too easy to get caught in this mindset—fearing that if they take their foot off the pedal everything will come crashing down.

Fear of failure is a terrible reason to take your business to the next level.

However, if you are thinking of restructuring to remove yourself from the day-to-day duties of running the business, that is a totally different story.

Chasing The Money?

One of the biggest mistakes you can make is getting caught up in *chasing the money*. There is only one way to get money—people have to give it to you. The key to successful growth is in the motivation of the leader. The group will reflect the attitude of the leader.

If your leadership is based on delivering high-quality service to your clients, you will attract those with the same focus—good, honest employees with only the best interests of the company and its clients in mind.

On the flip side, if you are growing a business that is focused solely on getting the most money from your customers, then you will attract money-driven employees. What do you think the results will be like from those employees?

You Want A Bigger Boat?

I spent some time with Steve, a medium-sized builder. He had started franchising his business about five years before we met, but only had around 20 franchises in the network.

Earlier still, he had been a franchisee in a large building franchise network and had been very successful in that business.

Because of his success he decided to break out of that network and start his own brand. He was very confident in his abilities to be a *franchisor*, and in his eyes he already had results. He had grown by one new franchisee every three months. And—he said all his franchisees were going well.

He was looking for a *business coach* to help him expand his small network of franchisees into a national brand in both

Australia and New Zealand; within three years. I was there to talk to him and see if I could help him reach his goals.

Let me say this—I completely understand that everyone is motivated by different goals. As part of my coaching process, I ask all my clients about their goals. And honestly, Steve's answers surprised me and even shocked him a bit.

His answer consisted of two parts. Firstly, he answered: *"I want a bigger boat than my old boss."*

Wait. What?

My response, after I got over my surprise, *"There are lots of other ways to get the money to buy a bigger boat, there must be another reason?"*

He answered: *"No, I want a bigger boat than him! My old boss is nothing more than a bogan with cash, if he can do it then I can do it better."* (*Bogan* is Australian slang for an uncouth or unsophisticated person regarded as being of low social status).

I should point out his ex-franchisor is the one of the biggest building franchisors in the Southern Hemisphere. They have large numbers of franchisees and have been in business for over 20 years. They build a lot of homes every year.

Getting a bigger boat than a someone in a business of that size might be tough ... he could be getting a bigger boat as we speak anyway?"

That being said, Steve did have a very valid point about being able to do some things better than the *other guy*.

Some of their practices really could stand to be improved upon and he certainly did have the abilities to do so.

However, if he honestly looked at the overall comparison between a long-term established business and his fledging franchise system, the results would definitely not be in his favour—they were outperforming him on most levels.

What's Going On Under The Surface?

Confidence and a competitive nature are vital attributes for any business owner wanting to go to the next level. Being brave enough to take a huge chance is big part of what drives many budding entrepreneurs. Fortune does truly favour the brave.

The problem in Steve's case was the ego that he was using to motivate himself. It was all about self-interest. He really just wanted to *beat* his old franchisor. *I don't know for sure what his old franchisor did to cause Steve's animosity towards him, but it must have been pretty awful.*

It was true some of Steve's systems were better than the old systems. But the bottom line was that he had really only re-engineered his old franchisors systems. At least, that's how I saw his system.

The biggest challenge he was facing in his business was the slow recruitment of his franchisees. He was spending good money on marketing for new franchisees.

He had about 30 new franchisee enquiries each month, not bad for a business with only 20 franchisees.

The real problem became clear rather quickly though—only one person joined his group every three months. That is only one out of every 90 new enquiries that converted to a new franchisee.

Not a very good conversion rate for anyone.

There was obviously something very wrong with his recruitment system. When I asked him about his recruitment process he said it all depended on whether they were *tyre kickers* or not. (A *tyre kicker* is salesperson slang for a buyer who is merely looks at many cars with no intention to actually buy one).

In my experience, this derogatory term is most often used by under-performing salespeople who blame the potential buyer for their poor results.

Apparently, one of his office administration people would take the first enquiry and only if they *sounded like good ones* to her, would she pass them on to Steve. If she didn't like the sound of them, or if she was busy, she would simply send them a brochure in the mail.

This clearly was not a professional franchise recruitment system. Untrained office staff evaluating his potential new franchisees from a quick phone call and a *gut instinct* seemed foolish, and frankly, disrespectful to the potential franchisees as well as the franchising industry as a whole.

I told him that in 20 years of being involved in franchise sales, I still cannot tell the good candidates from the bad ones based on a phone call. And that there was certainly no way an office administrator had the powers to read the future at that level.

I pointed out that I had sold more franchisees in my first three months of commencing franchising than he had done in five years, and that this attitude simply would not work. Steve's reasoning was that he had better things to do than waste time and money on those callers who weren't going to end up buying anything from him. He honestly felt that it was a waste of time to talk to customers that didn't buy?

Okay ...

I asked him about the sales system he had in place to sell homes. For the most part, he did have a system for this, but it ran pretty much parallel to that of his old franchisor. He thought it was different when he was selling franchises than when he was selling the actual houses.

They May Not Buy Today

Let me tell you, there are a lot of people who enquire about your *product,* no matter what it is, that will not buy immediately. They may buy tomorrow, they may buy next week, next month, or even next year.

Are you honestly willing to consider all of them a waste of your time simply because they didn't buy TODAY?

If you do... you may just be the best salesperson your competition has got. Because, using Steve as an example, most everyone will buy a house at some point. Operating the way Steve was operating insured his potential customers would go to the competition instead.

Not to mention, that his existing franchise systems were not giving confidence and direction to the families who were looking to join his network. His own self-interest had contaminated his entire business system.

The problem with Steve's business was that he created it from a completely selfish idea—to buy boats, aircraft, and flashy cars. He saw his business as a way to get the expensive toys he wanted to play with. He spent little to no time developing the systems in his business that would work for his potential franchisees and their clients.

Steve's primary interest in money so he could buy a bigger boat was reflected in the vibe he sent to his potential franchisees. I know we're talking about franchisees here but how do you think Steve treated the people who enquired about buying houses from him? I suspect the same.

I had the systems that could have put Steve's business on the right track to becoming a high-level franchisor. I didn't end up working with him though—I'm not much of a boat guy, honestly.

What Drives You?

For me, swallowing my pride when I was a young, 20-something year old dad, and learning the skills I needed to make my own car cleaning business a success completely changed my life and the lives of my family.

Throughout my 20 years of working with franchisees, I was always driven by the desire to share the dream of helping family businesses really work for their families. We used franchising to educate and lead thousands of family businesses to small business success.

Once you deliver the dream, the money will follow.

If you decide you want to grow your business to the next level, you must first take the time to make a definite decision about on where you want your business journey to end.

Then make the plan, take consistent action towards your dream business, and get the help you need to make those dreams a reality.

And remember:

"Chase the dream, not the money!"

The Gold

- The question is do you take your business to the next level? Is it worth the risk?

- Stop and take the time to make a definite decision about where you want your business journey to end.

- Fear of failure is a terrible reason to take your business to the next level, but if you want to restructure and remove yourself from the day-to-day duties of running the business, that is a different story.

- One of the biggest mistakes you can get caught up in is chasing money for money sake.

- Confidence and a competitive nature are vital attributes for any business owner wanting to go to the next level. Being brave enough to take the risk is big part of what drives the budding entrepreneur.

- The money will follow after you deliver the dream.

- "Chase the dream, not the money!"

Chapter 21
The *Magic* Of Growth
By Systemization

You can build a national network or a one-man band business that achieves all the goals for your family by systemization. No matter where you want to take your business there is a *magic* in systemization that can make your goals a reality.

What do I mean by *systemization*? I'm talking about taking all the pieces that make your business work, laying them out in front of you, and arranging them in a simple, easy-to-follow plan. Simply put, your documented systems are the building blocks of your business.

Systemization gives you the leverage to step away from the day-to-day tasks associated with running your business. The systems empower others to recreate the same level of performance as you do, over and over again.

No matter which service business you are in, the systems themselves can develop into a separate and valuable intellectual property if you want them to.

Proven business systems that can make money for others are in high demand throughout the world.

The traditional form of modernisation in business systems is of course franchising.

Franchising has revolutionised the small business world over the last 50 years. Franchising uses systems to empower small business owners to deliver a consistent level of professionalism to the customers.

Customers like knowing what they are going to get, no matter where they shop. The security of a big brand and the personalised service of the independent business owner combined in one place is a winner. Franchising works for the franchisor, franchisee and the customers.

Think about it—hamburgers and fries, your favourite cup of coffee, or the hotel you like most to stay in all became household names as they revolutionised the franchising industry.

There is no doubt that over the 50 years, small business owners have had a much higher success rate in a network with an experienced franchisor in their industry. There are three key areas in which a proven franchise system has been the most effective structure to deliver to small business owners the systemization that positively impacts their business.

These *three key systems* are vital for the long-term growth of any small business. If you plan to use the magic of systemisation to grow your business I highly recommend you learn the lessons from my last 25 years in franchising.

1—Training Systems

Initial training systems are the first place to start.

Systematically train your people exactly how you want them to do the job. A step-by-step process from the very beginning will make sure they understand what to do and how to do it— your expectations will be very, very clear.

The first introduction that any new team member has to your business has a huge long-term impact on how much of an impact they have on your business. Give them your effective habits before they contaminate the business with their amateur habits. These training systems should cover every part of the business.

Ongoing training systems will maintain the growth of both your people and your business. Build a system that evaluates the training needs of every member of your team. I recommend a half-day of training every month, a full day each quarter, and an annual 2-day event.

Initial and ongoing training systems are the foundations to the success of any business. Your business won't keep growing without systems that keep educating your staff.

2—Marketing Systems

I like to think of marketing efforts as the seeds that grow the business. All great franchise systems have truly great marketing systems. The key is they expect everyone to participate in those systems. Unlike corporate structures which take this responsibility away from their employees, successful franchisors empower their *business owners* with the tools to grow their own businesses.

This gives the business owner control of their own destiny.

There is nothing more insulting for a business owner than being treated like an employee. The opposite can also be true, empowering your employees with the marketing tools that they need to make a positive contribution to the business can give them full buy in.

Build marketing systems that work on every level of your business.

3—Support Systems

Things can and will go wrong in every business. Even the most finely tuned machines experience hiccups every so often.

All sorts of things can happen—sometimes people can just go off track, they lose focus, or miss a step, medical issues arise, and personal issues come up all the time. You never know what might happen or the impact it will have on your business. You must be prepared for the unexpected.

Your support systems will help you stay on track no matter what may happen. They are the key to your survival. Coaching and support systems that help evaluate where the business is at and how to get back on track are vital.

If you have a solid system in place, any one of your team-mates can step in and help out when needed. Even when it's a simple thing like sending a written quote to a client, or something more complicated like managing a new client through their first service.

Just because you are in business for yourself doesn't mean you want to be all alone in it. Support systems are the life line for all business owners.

The *Magic*

If you want to get the magic of systemisation working in your business, you will need to guarantee that training, marketing, and support systems are the foundations on which you build. These rules apply no matter what level you plan to grow your business to. It is true the bigger the business the larger and more detailed these systems will be.

It may seem like I am a big proponent of franchising. There is no doubt that franchising has changed the world. There are many excellent franchise business systems out there. Legends of franchising such as *McDonalds, Starbucks* and *Hilton* all have one thing in common—they have amazing systems.

No matter where you are in the world you know you can expect consistency within these brands. And that is very comforting.

There really are many areas where franchising is the *best* way to grow your business, but you may also find it to be outdated in your industry.

The real question is, *"Is franchising still the most effective way to get the key systems to their small business owners?"*

There was a franchising revolution, but that was nearly 25 years ago. I know, I was part of it. Most people knew nothing about franchising. They had heard of *McDonalds* but were unaware of *lower cost to enter business* systems.

We toured regional centres educating people about the benefits of our franchise network. It worked like a charm— the personal contact educated everyone, and we grew at an unbelievable rate.

The Master Franchisor

It was 1997 and face-to-face contact was the best way to deliver our proven systems to our people. People contact was vital in the service industry to deliver our training, support, and marketing systems.

With this in mind, we developed a Master Franchise regional system to deliver high-level support services to our franchisees. A Master Franchisor invests in the rights of a franchise system in a partial geographical area. They effectively act as the franchisor in their area.

In our case, the Master Franchisor would have a region and

the rights to develop the six home services systems. They would make their income from the sale of franchises and the ongoing fees.

Our franchisees needed the close, personal support, training, and marketing in their local area that their Master Franchisor could offer them. We couldn't be in every region giving them that face-to-face support.

So, we chose a franchisor in their region to act as the Franchisor on our behalf. The regional master system was a necessity at the time and it worked very well when the master franchisor followed the systems.

Everything Changes

Then the world changed—a new revolution was born called The Internet! The rules changed, new tools were born, and some people weren't prepared for the speed of that change. Actually, some people are still living in the good old days of the last century.

It was the year 2000 and the Internet Revolution was just beginning to make a huge impact on the traditional marketing mediums. But I didn't know that it was going to trigger a revolt within my own business.

Each year at *James Home Services*, we had an Annual General Meeting (AGM) that took place over a two-day period. We would educate our people, celebrate their successes, and I would reveal the plans for the coming year.

I could see the exact impact the Internet was having on our marketing. We had a system that tested and measured our marketing impact and at the time, *Yellow Pages*® was our biggest spend for service enquiry generation.

We were spending over $1 million dollars each year on *Yellow Pages* advertising and the cost was growing every year.

The franchisees loved the *Yellow Pages*.

When they were asked where they thought their work was coming from, most of our franchsees would say, "All my work comes from the *Yellow Pages!*" For years they were right.

The *Yellow Pages* peaked in 1998 at 89% of our service enquiries. In the same year, less than 5% of our service enquiries came from the internet, but that was a rapid jump from under 1% the year before. This was enough for me to start to test and measure this new *thing* called the Internet.

As the franchisor we started to run some new *modern* internet market strategies. Simply put, we built a series of websites that were designed to be search friendly. Today this is common place but in the year 2000 in was cutting edge stuff.

We tested and measured, got expert advice, and improved the systems. Not only did they work, but new internet marketing systems worked better than the *old school* traditional marketing.

The Results By The End Of 2000?

Yellow Pages dropped from 89% to 45% of service enquiries and the Internet made a rapid jump from 5% to 48% of our service enquiries. That is a 43% increase in only *TWO YEARS!*

The spend on *Yellow Pages* was $1,000,000 and the Internet spend was a mere $80,000. Yes—you read that right ... a $1 million price tag for 45% of our new business inquiries, and an $80,000 price tag for 48% of them. How does that make sense?

Now, imagine what would happen if we invested the *Yellow Pages* money into the Internet?

This internet revolution was a remarkable tool in marketing for the service industry. The results were truly amazing. I made the decision to jump on this wave. I thought the results were so amazing that everyone would be just as excited about it as I was. Ummmm ... I was wrong.

The Big Surprise

Apparently, not everyone is into revolutions. When I presented this exciting plan that moved our marketing away from the *Yellow Pages* and towards the Internet Revolution, I was shocked at the reaction.

I honestly expected a standing ovation from my franchisees and master franchisors. It was a marketing plan that gave our businesses modern systems that were better, cheaper, and yet, exponentially more effective than the old systems that everyone was accustomed to.

I found out very quickly at that AGM, that most people *DO NOT* like change. In fact, will dig their toes in if change happens too quickly for their personal preference.

The backlash was shocking! A couple of *Rebel Master Franchisees* even organised a meeting with franchisees with an agenda to stop the planned move into internet marketing. They actually paid lawyers to send threatening letters claiming the move would *destroy* their businesses.

It is now history. The Internet has changed the world in countless ways. Well, I ignored the legal threats and we experienced a boom for our businesses.

The fact remains that it was a good decision to get into Internet marketing because it changed everything. Otherwise, we would have been left behind. Instead, we were on the tip of the Internet wave watching other people trying to catch up.

Our businesses all thrived on the backs of these new marketing systems. The network kept growing, our franchisees had a marketing system that kept evolving. If anything, it proved our systems to improve the systems actually worked.

Now I see service industry franchising is becoming as old school as the *Yellow Pages*. The reality is that the Internet now has many platforms that can deliver training, marketing, and support systems much more effectively and to a larger audience than tradition franchising platform can. The current service franchise systems are built around Master Franchisor structures that are slow to react to change plus it adds an extra cost layer of management that is no longer required.

Outside of the *brand name* that comes with franchising, the intellectual property that most service franchise systems are built on is common knowledge on the internet. Many of the franchisors and master franchisors have simply bought the rights, have no personal intellectual property to bring to the game, and merely add a level of management that is not only outdated but frankly, unnecessary, and no longer needed.

The internet has certainly changed the way we all connect. However, some things never change. Having business systems that work will always have value. For many businesses franchising is still the best way to grow.

You can now share your systems with a world-wide market. The magic of growth by systemization for service business is in the power of the new tools that the internet can provide to them.

Build your systems and share them with the world. Magic really can happen.

The Gold

- No matter where you want to take your business there is a *magic* in systemization that can make your goals a reality.

- The systems empower others to recreate the same level of performance in each aspect of your business, over and over again.

- Proven business systems that can make money for others are in high demand throughout the world.

- For the last 20 years, there is no doubt, small business owners have had a much higher success rate as part of a network run by an experienced franchisor in their industry.

- There was a franchising revolution, but that was nearly 25 years ago.

- The internet revolution is a remarkable tool for marketing any service industry.

- Not everyone is into revolutions.

- Service industry franchising is becoming as old school as the *Yellow Pages* was.

- Many franchisors and master franchisors have merely bought rights. They have no personal intellectual property to bring to the game and only add a management level that is no longer needed.

- The internet has certainly changed the way we all connect. Some things never change, business systems that work will always have value.

- You can now share your systems with a world-wide market. The magic of growth by systemization for service businesses now is in the power of the new tools that the internet provides.

Chapter 22
Keeping Up the Pace

Okay, so you've decided to take another leap of faith. You've decided to push your business to the next level. You have got a clear goal in mind; systems that are proven and documented; you have wins on the board; you know you can do this! Well, you think you can anyway, right?

Then your biggest enemy comes in—*self-doubt*, and boy does it take hold. You suddenly can't think of anything but how hard it was getting started. You have gained loads of confidence from the success you've had up this this point, but do you really want to take the risk of losing what you have already achieved?

Do you have the ability to lead this show? Most likely at the moment the answer is no ...

It may feel a little like getting a new Formula One race car at this stage. It is this amazing piece of machinery that can go as fast and as hard as any vehicle on the planet. This is as good as a car can get. Then you get handed the key but wait ... you have to drive it?

The first corner is terrifying, you doubt that you will even get past this point. The speed in the straight is beyond anything you have ever experienced. It is both exhilarating and petrifying.

You suddenly come to the realisation that you are going to have to improve your skills in order to keep pace with the vehicle you have created, or you are likely going to crash and burn.

Growing With Your Business

Many business owners struggle with a fast-growing business because they are not open to learn the new skills needed to grow their businesses. Building the awesome machine that your business has become is only the start of your journey. The development of your own skills is vital to the management of your growing, successful business.

If you are using your systems effectively, you should begin moving yourself away from the day-to-day details of individual jobs and into leadership and higher-level management skills. This may take some skills you don't currently possess and that is perfectly normal.

I know for myself one my biggest challenges in the early days of my business was my own self-image. I was a horse trainer who started a car cleaning business. Then at 27 years old, I was suddenly a franchisor.

I even had trouble describing exactly what I did to get where I was ... sometimes I still do ...

I went from cleaning cars myself every day to sitting in an office. The way I dressed changed from a work uniform to shirt and tie and boy was it a culture shock. But my uniform change was a trigger that made me understand just how important it was that I grow along with the business. It was clear to me that to grow my business, I was going to have to learn some new skills—and quickly.

The first thing I had to do was take a good, hard look in the mirror and figure out in what areas I was most lacking in order to achieve my grand plan.

Figuring Out The Skills You Need

What were the things I did not know enough about? Let's start at the beginning:

- Selling franchises
- Marketing my business to a larger market
- How to best utilize multiple forms of media
- Business coaching

Oh boy ... my list seemed very daunting—I was going to have to learn to do all of these things if I wanted my business to succeed. And, I was going to have to learn them pretty fast!

A daunting list of lacking skills is pretty scary and honestly, it may be enough to stop many business owners in their tracks. It is really hard to take a look at yourself and be that honest about your shortcomings. Most people like to concentrate on the things they do well, not the things they don't do so well.

Here's the thing, I had 100% buy in into our mission. We were designing the best family-friendly home services franchise system in the country. I had already learned so much, why not learn more?

Learn, Learn, And Learn Some More

Lucky for me I had always been an avid reader, I read every day. Books were the logical place to start, so that is exactly what I did—I started reading. In the early franchising years, I bought lots of books and read them all.

I believe books are still the best education tool ever invented. There are experts on every single subject in the world and frankly, most of them love to write about what they are an expert in. Ummmm ... kind of like I'm doing right now, I suppose.

Your willingness to learn new things will open up huge opportunities for you and your business in the years ahead. If you want to grow with your business, it is vital to be open to admitting to yourself that there are skills that you need to improve upon or perhaps things you know nothing about and need to learn from scratch.

Actively search out those who can educate you in those particular areas. In today's world the internet gives us a very powerful tool to access those who can educate us in every field imaginable. Use it to your advantage!

While it is true that some self-proclaimed *Internet Gurus* out there have no real results so do your due diligence, investigate each one you are interested in and you will find the ones that are the real deals.

The power of a good mentor is hard to match. A mentor who has been there and done that (no matter what that may be) can take you and your business to unbelievable heights. This mentor could be a specialist in one particular field.

I personally have had specialist mentors in public speaking, writing, blog content, internet marketing and branding, personal fitness, as well as business and business coaching. Each individual educated me in their area of expertise and added great value to my skills.

Finding The Right Coach

Over the years I have met many individuals who refuse to grow with their business. They are usually caught up in their own delusional belief that they are *all good*. The only way to stop kidding yourself is to set your ego aside and honestly evaluate your own results. Take an honest look at what you are doing. Ask those around you for feedback.

If you have areas in which you lack skills, you will quickly figure them out.

When I first became a franchisor, I had absolutely no public speaking skills. I was terrified speaking in front of a group and had no idea what I was doing. Obviously, this was going to be a problem. I knew this, but every month I had to run a series of meetings, the business was growing at a rapid rate, the meetings were growing every month. I was getting very quickly out of my depth.

I needed help, so I went in search of a presenting coach and that's when I found Rod. Rod is a professional speaker, and he is really good at what he does. He is honest, pragmatic and knows his stuff, perfect for a coach really. Rod and I did a road trip to all the meetings for a month. He gave me plenty of feedback, some good and some not so good of course. But everything he told me was right on target.

It is vital that you have mentors that give you honest feedback, there is no point having someone who keeps telling you how *great* you are when it is simply not true—you will not grow that way.

There are a lot of business coaches out there who believe they get paid to stock the egos of their business clients. Do yourself a favour and stay away from these Gurus, they are a total waste of your hard-earned money.

Rod also gave me a systematic structure to improve my presentation. He recommended I record all my presentations and listen to how I was performing. I truly hated this, I found my own presentations terrible. I couldn't stand the sound of my own voice. But I did it for ten years and you know what? It worked, I really was my own toughest critic.

Over the years, I improved my presentations and my delivery, I got truly comfortable speaking in front of a large group. I grew from being a terrified learner to a true professional, but it did take ten years of evaluation, education, and implementation and practice.

Invest in your personal grow and you will be able to keep pace with your business. The success of your business will inevitably cause you some growing pains. It's okay ... it's a good problem to have—when you realize your business is getting so successful that you can no longer fill all the gaps by yourself.

If you are lucky the success will pressure you into developing new skills that you thought you may never have been able to do. The personal skills you develop will be with you for life.

The Gold

- You have wins on the board, you know you can do this. Well you think you can? Then self-doubt starts to take hold.

- Many business owners struggle with a fast-growing business because they are not open to learn the new skills needed to grow with their business.

- This list of skills lacking can be very daunting and may stop many business owners in their tracks.

- The power of a good mentor is hard to match. A mentor who has been there and done that can take you and your business to unbelievable heights.

- I have met many individuals who refuse to grow with their business. Caught up in their own delusional belief that they are all good.

- Invest in your personal grow and you will be able to keep pace with your business.

Chapter 23
The Best Game In Town

There is no doubt that running your own business is absolutely the best game in town. There is no other game that can give you as much fun, excitement, opportunity, and reward! Running a successful business will change your life.

It will require you to:

- Decide where you want to go.

- Venture out of your comfort zones.

- Have a willingness to learn new things.

- Be disciplined and stick to these proven systems.

- Be willing to ask for help and accept it along the way.

- And, most importantly, take constant action.

Most people are averse to taking risks. This is why making the decision can be the hardest step.

Your own self-doubt may get it the way. Family and friends may even be *warning* you to be very careful. The news constantly covers only the bad news about businesses failing. With all of this in mind, being fearful is an understandable way to feel.

For many it is difficult to make that decisions on long-term goals because of the constant fear of failure. But doing nothing is the biggest failure of all.

If you have always dreamed of being your own boss, then decide to live your dream. If you love dogs, gardening, yoga, or hairdressing and you love giving great service, then you are on the right track. You just have to decide that you want to have a successful business and then do it—make your dream come true. No one is going to do this for you!

There will be personal comfort zones that you will have to get through. I know I been uncomfortable with something for most of my business life. Every time you try something new, it will feel uncomfortable. Once you get beyond these comfort zones you will also achieve your greatest life victories.

If you want to be successful in your business, you must be willing to learn. This is can be difficult for many people.

I have seen many business owners so worried that they aren't smart enough to learn. This can go back to their schooling history or the conditioning from society or family.

If you are told something enough times, you may actually start to believe it. You have to open yourself up to learning and challenge the belief that

You should know anything.

The principles in this book have been proven thousands of times. So, take them on and learn them until they become second nature. You have to be first open to the learning and use that education to build your personal confidence.

It will take true discipline to stick to these proven systems. All professionals learn to stick to their systems especially under pressure. To make the transition to professional business owner you do have to make sure you to stick to these systems. The systems have been proven, they work in the market place.

Don't second guess them, just do it and watch the results.

Learning to ask for help may sound a bit new age or you may even think of it as a sign of weakness. I believe the opposite is the true. A pragmatic business owner knows that to deal with a problem as quickly as possible can oftentimes require the help of others.

I have had a mentor, a presenting coach, a long-term business coach, a writing coach, and even a digital marketing coach throughout my career. I understand my world is changing and I have to evolve to keep up with the changes. If you reach out and learn from the right people, you can learn anything you require. I believe you will be surprised yourself, if you have the willingness to ask for help.

But most importantly you absolutely must take consistent action. It has to be consistent with the systems that are leading towards your final business. Get up each day, go to work and do what you are supposed to be doing. Just be careful not to *out-think* yourself—it is more common than you think ...

I used to coach a lovely fellow named Bob. Bob was a great carpet cleaner and pest control operator. He had a long career as a military serviceman—after 20 years in the air force, he made the move to get out and started his own business.

His business was very up and down. It went from great weekly turnover to low turnover which was totally freaking Bob out. He had had a consistent income for 20 years and now he had no idea what his income would be next week.

Bob was very worried. When I say worried, I mean 24/7 worried. Even when he had a big week, he was already worried about next week because it was certainly going to be less.

He took worrying to the next level. He had built his own spreadsheet that tracked just how inconsistent his turnover income was. I spent hours studying his spreadsheet. Then he would invest hours in worrying about his next week turnover.

When I sat down to do the business coaching with Bob, he told me what he thought his problem was. He pointed out all the above. He clearly believed that his inconsistent income was the problem.

I asked a simply question. "What are you doing about it?"

Bob's answer? He pointed to his spreadsheet then said, "I'm worrying about it!" He was worrying so much that he couldn't sleep at night, he would lay in bed for hours worrying about next week's income. He spent weekends studying his perfectly neat, up-to-date spreadsheets trying to predict *"How bad next week was going to be!"*

Bob was putting an awful lot of energy into worrying about what was wrong with his business. He was making himself busy, but he wasn't taking action that would lead towards the long-term business goals.

Worrying is NOT action, it is a negative thought which led Bob to take avoidance action. This was a life habit of Bob, to quote him *he was a worrier, always had been.*

My advice to Bob was to stop wasting his life worrying and to focus instead on his systems. He needed to take action and do what he was required to do to build his business.

Simply put, he had to do *Step #1* every day, *Market his business daily.* He was ignoring the first step and replacing it with his own *worrying systems* that did nothing but undermine his success. Bob stopped worrying, (I gave him two weeks leave from worrying, he thought he could do without worrying for a couple weeks) and he took action.

He followed our systems and did *Step #1—Marketing every day* and it worked! It was a turning point for Bob in his business and in his life. He decided that he could take permanent leave from worrying and replace it with a new habit of taking positive action. He lived the dream, he became a very successful business owner.

There is no doubt running your own business is absolutely the best game in town.

Running a successful business will change your life. You can do this, so do it.

The dream is yours, you are the one who can make it a reality. Now go make it happen ... develop the business of your dreams!

References

* Blanchard. K. (2002). *Whale Done: The Power of Powerful Relationships.* Hodder & Stoughton General Division; 1st edition

* Covey, S. R. (1989). *The 7 Habits of Highly Effective People: Powerful Lessons of Personal Change.* Simon & Schuster

* Gerber, M. (1986). *The E-Myth: Why Most Small Businesses Don't Work and What To Do About It.* HarperCollins Publishers Inc

* Johnson, Dr S. (1998). *Who Moved My Cheese? An Amazing Way to Deal With Change In Your Work and In Your Life.* Ebury Publishing

* Ries, A & Trout, J. (1981). *Positioning: The Battle for Your Mind.* McGraw-Hill Education - Europe

* Robbins, A. (1991). *Awaken The Giant Within: How To Take Immediate Control of Your Mental, Emotional, Physical and Financial Destiny.* CreateSpace

Acknowledgments

I want to firstly acknowledge of five amazing children. Hayden, Cameron, Nadine, Rohan and Luke. You inspire me to always chase the dream, even when life throws challenges in the way. We have been through our share of hardship and challenges but when it matters we have always stood strong for each other. The love of the family is the foundations of life.

To my Dad, *Johnny James,* (As everyone in our home town of Maitland, NSW, calls him) . Thank you for always being there and always being positive and supportive. Not once in my life did you said, "That won't work!"

You taught me that everyone makes mistakes but that is just the way it is. All you have to do is get up and have another go.

You are a great dad, good mate, Great Granddad ,so smart and wise that I don't know what I would have done without in my life. Family tell me they look at me and see you in me, I'm honoured. I love you Dad.

To my Mum, You taught me to be patient ,caring and forgiving. No one is perfect but people can learn and change. Your lifetime commitment to the family is something I aspire too. You always saw the good in all your kids.

You showed me that anyone can change if they take accountability. You have always been a loving Mum, Nanny and now Great Nanny. I love you Mum.

To my sister Katherine (Flo)and I have been friends as much as siblings for our whole lives. Leaning on each other when things were tough and also combining our talents to achieve huge milestones in those early days of *James Home Services.*

To my Business Coach of 20 years, Vac Ubl, who was my business coach before anyone else even thought of the idea of a business coach. Thanks for being a great sounding board, adviser and sharing this journey with me. No one could have never predicted where the journey would lead at the being.

To all the *James Home Services* franchisees who I worked with over the many years. I learnt as much form you as I taught. It was an honor to lead the *James Home Services* network from my one-man car cleaning business to a national brand. I still find it amazing what we achieved.

Thanks to Andrew Priestley, my editor and publisher on this book. You have been patient but also have kept me on the program. Funny how the second book has been more *uncomfortable* than the first. Your understanding and direction got us to the finish line.

About Robert M James

Robert M James started his business career, at the age of 22, as a horse trainer and breaker. As a young dad of two sons, he started a mobile car cleaning business to help feed his growing family. Business wasn't easy in the early days.

"I really didn't know, what I didn't know! I thought, if I was a great horseman or a good car cleaner, the clients would just come to me. I was so wrong, there are so many other business skills I needed to be able to grow a successful service business."

But with pragmatism, determination and an open mind he learnt the new skills needed and his car cleaning business evolved into a huge success.

By the age of 27 he commenced to franchise network, *James Home Services,* which grew into a 400-strong network franchise system servicing over $20 million in services yearly.

The proven ideology behind this book is the same that empowered countless service business owners to build extraordinary service businesses over a 20 year period.

Robert business coached and educated countless franchisees to business success in many different service industry niches.

If you are ready to succeed then this book will help you:

- Build your own extraordinary service business.

- Learn the proven nine foundation secrets that built a national franchise network.

- Decide what service business you should do.

- Design your own brand.

- Successfully and effectively market your service business.

- Learn professional sales and quoting skills.

- Learn who to build a loyal profitable client base very quickly.

- Continue to deliver gold medal professional level services *every time* to *every client.*

- Use the magic of systemisation to grow the business of your dreams.

- Grow a business that suits your goals.

- Live the dream of being a successful business owner.

"Everything in this book is proven to work in the market place where it matters. Follow the proven secrets and your business can grow into whatever you choose. I know, I have seen thousands of families grow extraordinary business."

If you have always dreamed of being in your own business in the service industry but didn't know where to start then this book has the answers for you.

If you have an existing business and it could be performing even better then either way, this book is chock full of business gold that will take your business to the next level amazingly quickly.

There is nothing more rewarding than running your own successful services business. It is the best game in town.

Contact Robert M James

- https://balance.enterprises/contact/
- https://www.linkedin.com/in/robert-james-1b44b6ab/
- https://twitter.com/jamesmaster99
- chasethedream@bigpond.com

Lightning Source UK Ltd.
Milton Keynes UK
UKHW021040060223
416538UK00017B/2367